Light Nights and Wet Feet

Light Nights and Wet Feet

A Walk Through Modern Scotland

Robert Grundstein

Authors Choice Press

San Jose New York Lincoln Shanghai

Light Nights and Wet Feet
A Walk Through Modern Scotland

Authors Choice Press
an imprint of iUniverse.com, Inc.

For information address:
iUniverse.com, Inc.
5220 S 16th, Ste. 200
Lincoln, NE 68512
www.iuniverse.com

Original cover art by Deborah Roundtree.
Cover design and map pages by Claudia Carlson.

ISBN: 0-595-14115-3

Printed in the United States of America

To Professor N.D. Grundstein; an original and generous mind.

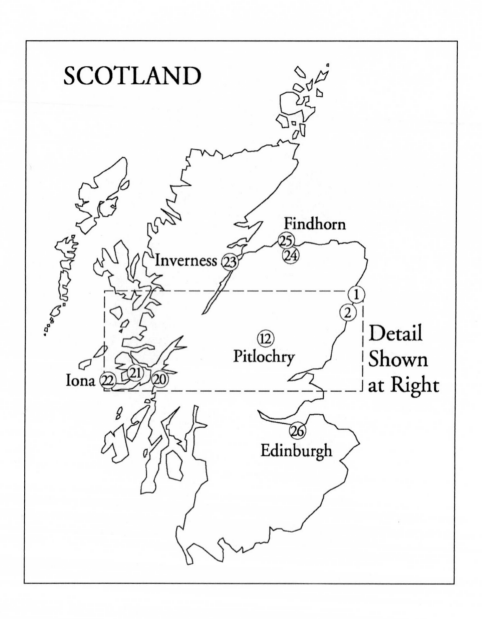

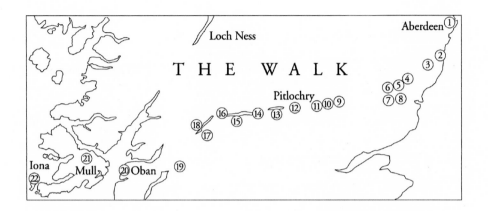

T H E   W A L K

Loch Ness

Aberdeen

Pitlochry

Iona   Mull   Oban

1) Aberdeen
2) Stonehaven
3) Drumlithie
4) Fettercairn
5) Edzell
6) Brigend
7) Careston
8) Brechin
9) Glenisla
10) Blacklunans
11) Kirkmichael
12) Pitlochry (to London by train, Yorkshire by car, back to Pitlochry by train)
13) Loch Tummel

14) Kinloch Rannoch
15) Loch Rannoch
16) Rannoch Station
17) Rannoch Muir
18) Loch Laidon
19) Dalmally
20) Oban
21) Island of Mull
22) Iona (back to Oban)
23) Inverness (by bus)
24) Forres (by bus)
25) Findhorn (by bus)
26) Edinburgh (by bus)

Chapter One

Sometimes, you find yourself somewhere

"What the fook you waitin' for? Think we're a boos? Throw your kit in the back and hurry up."

I had been waiting for two hours when this car and its small trailer stopped fifty yards ahead of me. I thought it might be a joke so I walked slowly in anticipation of their quick departure and an obscene gesture. It didn't move and my pace only aggravated the two men from Newcastle in the car.

"*Christ*, ye take yer time."

I closed the door and noticed the silent driver and his older, crusty companion.

"What you been eatin' man? Garlic?" He stretched it out so it sounded like ga-a-h-lic.

"No, not me, and thanks for stopping."

"Smells like garlic."

I was on my way to Scotland.

I bumped from ride to ride and stood a while at the Scottish border where traffic passed indifferently and an overweight French family turned their thumbs down at the row of hitchhikers from the inside of their camp-mobile. A ruddy Scot finally stopped his overfilled car, and I sat squashed between the door and his silent girlfriend who dyed her hair an unwholesome looking black. He was a good fellow and offered cigarettes around while staring out the windshield through irises that looked like transparent blue candies. They were so clear I wondered whether they were effective for vision, but he drove without incident and worried over the best place to let me out.

In Edinburgh, I was dropped off in the southern part of the city. Instead of asking to be let out on the freeway, I let my curiosity lead me into the town. I knew I had to cross the Firth of Forth Bridge to get north, but I didn't know how once I was off the main highway. After I left the car I walked towards a bus stop and stood there, feeling exposed, and tried to get my pack out of the way of pedestrian traffic. Everyone here belonged to something. They were going home, or to work or to visit friends. I was unconnected, and felt that concentrated moment of fear which accompanies an irreversible commitment to an encounter with the unknown. The same question came into my mind as I stood there like a torn paper bag in South Edinburgh as after I have punched someone much larger than myself: "Should I have done that?"

I collected myself and went to a waiting bus. At the entrance the driver told me that he could take me downtown and I could continue north from there. As the bus made its way uptown in little units of stop and start I looked across at a boy in steel toed boots carrying a walking stick/weapon made from sections of pipe and wondered what he had in mind.

Edinburgh looked pretty civilized. As the bus passed streets along the route, you could look down them and see the heather and cliffs at the end of town. The city ended abruptly in contrast to L.A., where I lived, which seemed to end in Mexico. We crossed the river Dean and stopped in the middle of castle-like buildings. Edinburgh was like a large medieval city anchored by stone but accessible to nature. It was midsummer light and from its hills, one could see the Firth widen towards the ocean. Brass hardware adorned the black granite buildings and crowds of people filled the sidewalks. I wanted to linger but decided to go on to Aberdeen and dawdled over to a phone to get directions to the intercity bus terminal.

At the station people collected in the dreary waiting room which was dingy, but lacked the desolation and threat of violence that lurks in the bus stations of most large American cities. I roamed around and looked for something to eat in a mean little cafeteria with low ceilings and plastic seats. A selection of pies was displayed under orange heat lamps. Pies appeared to be central to Scotland, sort of the light meal equivalent to hot dogs in the U.S.. I stared at them in the orange glow of their private warming box. It was a little food world. The pies were flaky pastry cut in comfortable shapes and filled with beef, curry, cheese, or spinach. I bought a beef one and looked at it. It had a criss-cross pattern across the center and a folded crust around the edge, which looked like a little pastry curb. It looked homey and safe and I liked its heft in my hand. As I brought it towards my mouth for a bite, I saw the sheen of shortening and baked egg glaze on the surface. Several layers of crust compressed and the chopped meat filling pushed forward and expanded the part I pinched off between my teeth. There was the taste of onion, rich pastry and the depth of beef all at once. I wondered what kind of mentality created this and thought of cheery Northerners who work hard outdoors in an unfriendly climate and need the food equivalent of a hearth to greet and warm them. The pie was hearty and thoughtful; coarse and fine at the same time.

"Is there something in yer pie?" the man behind the counter brusquely asked.

"No, its fine."

"Yer starin' at it. Could you move along? People behind. It's not that interestin' anyway."

"Yes, of course."

A stout woman and her child pushed around me. The boy had on two sweaters and looked like a stuffed puppet. He grabbed three ice creams from the freezer display. His mother lurched forward.

"None now. Put them back."

She took two from him. He put one behind his back and crushed it so the wrapper distorted and cracked. His expression was of fear and exhilaration as his mother turned red in front of him.

"Aye, look what you've done, we'll have to buy it now."

She put her pudgy fingers into a change purse and counted out the precise amount while the boy looked into the small bag without remorse.

"I'll be tellin' your father, you might get a strap tonight."

"Can I have a fruit drink?" he asked.

"Have you been listenin' to me?" she screamed.

Her breath went past him like a small typhoon. His eyes opened wide as the wind went past his ears and he hid a smile. This was a small adventure for him. She turned and yanked him past the tables to the bus stands. The ice cream was almost accelerated out of his hand.

I contemplated my pie a bit more and chewed as I waited for the bus north. Wistfully, I finished the last bite and went out where I sat with a family on a bench. Blonde twins moved a doll back and forth and made little speaking noises for them.

"Would you like some tea?"

"Chocolate would be better."

"Chocolate and tea don't go."

"You always argue."

The parents sat there silently. They looked like working people although the father wore a tie. He stared out as if he didn't see anything. He had an unsentimental face that looked like it was made for hardship. Thin lips, loud blue eyes, and the permanent absence of self-pity.

My bus pulled out towards Aberdeen. We drove along fields of cereal grasses and the ocean. Long low hills to the west were patched in green and tan. People on the bus had quiet talks that consisted of quick bits of information exchange. The seats were too close together and I fidgeted. A drunken man reached for a young man seated next to his girlfriend.

"Off to Arbroath, eh Jimmy?"

"Hands to yourself," the boy said quietly. The connection with this man was part of a history he wanted to end.

"No, it doesn't have to be like that Jimmy."

His voice was small and private. His expression remained unchanged and he returned to his seat, from where he stared out the window. The boy turned away and an empty bottle of whiskey rolled into the aisle. No one picked it up until we arrived in Aberdeen.

In second grade, I decided that I wanted people to think I was from Texas. It was difficult, especially since I had known all the children since Kindergarten. Creating a new identity could be done, but no one believed the geography part of it. There was a quiet girl from North Dakota and some kids whose parents had moved from Appalachia. Other than that, everybody had spent their entire lives together. My first grade "My Life" report, given in front of forty children, listed my place of birth as Henry Ford Hospital, Detroit, Michigan. I was forgiven about the Texas thing, but I still wanted to be part of something larger and stirring. Would Roy Rogers and Dale Evans adopt me? No, that was my sister's fantasy. It wouldn't work anyway. Where would they ride the horses in Detroit? Palmer Park? On the sidewalk so our mother would say O.K.?

As I entered adolescence, we moved twice and my teenage environment was a preview of American adult life. Bad teachers made demands on us, which they weren't equipped to support. Ultimately we were taught to be subordinates in preparation for a place in consumer society. Variations in individual opportunity were heavily influenced by the professional status of a student's family. We learned despite our teachers, most of whom didn't like teaching or the students. Nothing held us together. Destinies were individual. Our beacon was competitive participation in economic life. Social interactions ran from the overtly hostile to homophobic comradeship. We were a horde, climbing over each other and spitting at the person below. Was this fear necessary? Life seemed based on it.

Jennifer Webb always walked home alone. Her family was Canadian of Scottish descent and her manner wasn't aggressive or partisan enough for the other eighth grade girls. Sometimes I would pass her on my way home and say hello. She was serene and had large breasts comfortably wrapped by a brown sweater. She spoke in mannered, polite tones and gave thoughtful answers to my questions about her life in Canada. I imagined she lived in a great quiet hall with silent grounds and stony grey skies. Her family would quietly acknowledge one another when they met, but they lived their lives in a tasteful, alone-togetherness sustained by the dignity and soft privacy of what they were. Maybe she would let me feel her breasts in this surreal place.

The Encyclopedia article for Canada ended with a cite that said, "See England, Scotland, Ireland, Wales. Also Highland Clearances." I thought the Dictionary would be easier so I flipped to Scotland. In the margin was one of those Dictionary illustrations of a man in a Kilt, a castle and further down, an imaginary Pict with a spear. It seemed obscure. I flipped back to Canada. If I knew some facts about it maybe I could impress Jennifer. I also hoped no one would see me with her.

I was fired from my attorney's job in Albuquerque N.M. the same week I closed on the purchase of a house there. Albuquerque is like a little foreign country in the middle of nowhere. It is ugly, hot, isolated and has a university with the second highest dropout rate in the country. After putting myself in the cesspool, I closed the door over me. I became lost. At my house my roommate had organized a party. I stirred my drink with my finger and contemplated my anxiety with disbelief.

"You don't look well."

I was staring at a red-haired girl who spoke with a brogue.

"Who are you?"

"A friend of Larry's. I'm Maureen."

"Where are you from?"

"Scotland, where else?" She looked at me as if my ignorance was not excusable.

"What are you doing here?"

"It's lovely here."

"What do you mean? It's filled with conventionalists, liars and small-minded imbeciles."

"It's a good place to be poor."

"Poor is never good, unless you like outrage, powerlessness and degradation."

"You're having a time. Is your drink not right?"

I stared at her for a moment. She wasn't pretty but projected goodwill and character strength. She waited for me to say something.

"What's your last name?"

"MacDonald." She spoke slowly and deliberately.

"Popular Scot name, like Campbell."

"No, not alike at all. I'll have you know the Campbells fought with the British against the Scots in several wars. MacDonald fought on the other side. As was proper." She bristled, then giggled.

What a foreigner. She had a sense of history and held non-commercial notions of belief and loyalty. After dealing with the attorneys in Albuquerque, I was sure right and wrong no longer existed. There was only risk assessment left and the person who lied best and last, won.

"What's it like in Scotland?"

"Kind of wet and it stays light in the summer."

"Where did you live?"

"Dunfermline, outside of Edinburgh. I went to University there. On a scholarship, mind you."

"Big deal."

"T'was a big deal, my father was a chauffeur. I was supposed to be really something."

She smiled at the irony of her life.

"What do you do now?"

"I cane chairs, like a Crofter."

"What's that?"

"A small cottage dweller. They're quaint."

"I think I heard of you. You're a friend of Sharon Harz. Right?"

"Sort of, she's mainly a woman good for sex. Not really my type."

"Sex is good!"

"Stop that! Come by for a whiskey if you don't mind some time. And mind your manners."

An erect person. She'd stab someone in the heart with a scissors if crossed. She couldn't be bought. I had been spending my time with people who only could be bought and who were also dull. Anthropologists sometimes say the people are the land. In Albuquerque it was true. The attorneys were overheated dirt. I looked around my backyard and wondered how I was going to pay for it until I fled from it.

———————

Aberdeen is a small city of rock. From the bus station it has the grim facade of a cold war espionage movie. My friend Laura and I walked through it as she gave me a tour. She lived here.

"It has the best economy in Scotland now, North Sea oil you know. Heaps of people are moving here. U.K. economy is shrinking fast. There are something like four hundred bankruptcies a week now in England."

We walked past "Fittdee" which was the old residence for the fishing community. It had low stone homes and wooden shacks built around courtyards.

"It's fashionable now. Things are expensive here. People even fix up the old drying shacks and use them."

We went on to Old Aberdeen, a stone settlement which includes the University and walked along its continuous structures of thick stone walls, enclosures and secluded yards. Despite its substance, it was not intimidating but private and cozy. Things were wide rather than tall and one could see the trees and gardens over many of the low walls. It was dark by the time we got back and downtown Aberdeen was filled with people visiting the pubs.

"It's odd being in a place where it gets dark at 10:30 P.M."

"That's the way it is in the north," said Laura, "Try to remember seventh grade science. Summer you know."

We met some friends of Laura's at a pub. Willy and his wife, Lavinia, were from Glasgow. Willy had the craggy face and jaw of a street fighter. Lavinia spoke quietly and measured people through her narrow eyes. The entire world seemed to be her potential adversary.

"How do you find our country?" asked Willy. His manner was surprisingly soft.

"I can't tell, I just got here. Everything looks like a castle though. You don't find places like Edinburgh in the states. And everyone sort of looks the same here. Not like twins, but they have a connection. In the U.S. you see faces you don't see here. Also, people don't get along so well. Lots of division along race in particular."

"It's tough here. Lots of violence, right around here," said Willy.

"In little Aberdeen?"

"Aye, I had to walk Laura's boyfriend home one night after he got drunk. We were right around the corner when someone with a knife tried to slash us. It was unprovoked."

"Why?"

"Can't say, that's what unprovoked means. Drunk looking for a fight, I guess."

"In major U.S. cities there are hundreds of murders each year," I offered.

"We have nothing like that, but the economy can't take everyone in the cities. Things are good in Aberdeen now. Wait 'til the oil pulls out."

"Things will fall then," said Lavinia, "Homes won't be so expensive."

"What are things like in America? I've often wanted to go to Arizona. I have read books on Indian Art. Those people seem to revere the Earth." Willy looked a little wistful.

"They are romanticized," I countered, "they can be pretty tough and were ruined by the Europeans. During the Indian rodeo in Albuquerque they will drink your beer while you're on the dance floor. The Pueblo Indians are interesting. They live near where I used to live in New Mexico. They have their own communities along the Rio Grande and in some cases live there like they have for hundreds of years."

"It's so open there," said Willy, "You could go where you want." He yearned to go.

"People do move a lot in America."

"Our neighbor lived at the same flat for thirty years. Her husband wanted to move a mile and a half away to a larger place. She said no. It was too far to move. She couldn't go one and a half miles," Lavinia laughed, "We like the places we know."

I looked around the pub. It was plain and square with lots of people who looked like they were in their sixties. Couples sat at tables and booths and made barely audible exchanges. Many of the men wore ties and the ladies wore makeup in deference to this modest social forum.

Laura and I walked back to her flat along a main street. The pubs were closing and the way was filled with clusters of people waiting for cabs. We passed lots of vomit.

"It's the big night out," explained Laura, "Go out, get pissed, have some Curry chips and blow it all on the street. That's your Friday."

The take-away shops were humming and private clubs with late hours and shirt and tie dress codes were queued up. Men argued with the bouncers who managed the doorways. People were impatient to get in. The places were jammed.

"Come on. Lets get a Doner Kebab. That's what you do," said Laura. I followed her bouncing curls down a hill.

We walked along a curved street to a well-lit shop. As we carried our food back up the hill, we passed a boy being sick half over a wall. One leg was extended along the ledge and his head was on the other side. His trailing leg remained on the sidewalk. The carousers and vomiters created a Celtic, Fellini scene of consumption and excess in the eerie twilight darkness. At Laura's flat we watched "The Swamp Thing" on late night television. After everyone fell asleep I looked at maps and planned for the beginning of my walk.

Chapter Two

Kindness of English

I started walking at Stonehaven, a small city just south of Aberdeen. The station was quiet as I got off the train. A little fanfare would have been nice, but on the other hand I didn't want to feel conspicuous as I hauled my pack up the stairs and tried to decide which way to head. It was five thirty in the afternoon. There were about four and a half hours of light left and I had no idea where I would sleep that night. At a deserted pub adjacent to the station, I asked for directions west and started out.

I walked tentatively up a street and around a traffic circle to a small road I would follow to Drumlithie, about ten miles away. I checked my shoes and adjusted the straps on the pack. They were fine. I felt like I was inching my way off the high dive. It was ridiculous to be so apprehensive. The road was clear for a mile. A bunch of skittish, black-faced sheep lurched away from the fence as I walked by in the grass. I felt better. We were all nervous.

As I passed the last municipal works of Stonehaven the area became totally rural. The wind blew east and the grass waved continuously. I felt I must observe now. I'm really in Scotland. Look! Scottish animals, Scottish grass, Scottish wind. Fifteen minutes later I walked by the small Kirktown outside of Stonehaven. A small turn in the road led to it and I entered the center of the town, which had about eight structures, the main one being the church and graveyard. The graveyard was tidy and fenced by stone. No one was around so I entered and looked at the markers. A lot of the stones mentioned relatives of the deceased who died in America or Canada. There was nothing much past 1720 and the original church had a caved-in roof.

A silent inn was next to the graveyard entrance and I leaned over the fence to look. Its country domesticity made me yearn to be inside it. The slate roof came low and was laid with thick, grey tiles. A worn stone path led to the entrance through a yard cloistered by small trees and hedges. Two ramshackle out buildings, which were older than the main house leaned against it, like children against a mother. Large oaks shaded the entire area. I didn't need anything but I had to put myself in the center of that environment. This silent place was so comfortable and orderly at the same time. I felt the substance of the earth connection created by the stone building materials. I knocked on the door and waited. No one answered, so I continued on in the yellow afternoon-like light.

As it grew dark I walked into Drumlithie. On the outskirts a man was shooting at gulls and the bullets spun through the branches above my head. I shouted and heard no acknowledgment. Another round whizzed past so I abandoned conversation and ran two hundred yards towards the center of town, slowed down and walked another hundred yards and stood in front of a large, silent pub with two entrances. I stared and tried to decide which one to take, then went in the right door which had a sign saying "Bar meals served all day." As I entered I felt like I was going into someone's house; there was no institutional feel about it. The design of the place was erect and angular. I walked into the stall-like foyer, pushed open a wood and glass door and turned left through another set of doors into the bar area. It was empty. The lounge adjacent to it was full of men muttering and laughing. I felt it was too intimate to interrupt so I sat in the deserted bar and asked the lady for a whiskey. The bar menu offered carbohydrates and starch. Chips, meat pies and various cold meats with mayonnaise referred to as salads.

A girl walked in wearing a cardigan sweater, a plaid skirt and flats. She looked like a prison matron but her manner was pleasant. I sat and drank my whiskey while the activity in the next room remained separate. I thought about how different this was from a bar in Indonesia or Mexico, where in the small villages everybody will sit at your table without being asked and the children will pull at your body hair out of curiosity. Familiarity is easy and privacy is not as paramount a social value. It wasn't unpleasant here though, and the domesticity of the place was ineradicable. They had urbanized tables with walnut veneer and bottles lined up behind the bar with professional portion controllers, but you couldn't take the home out of this place. I sat comfortably without speaking to anyone for an hour, and left.

By the time I was a mile out of town it was twilight and I was looking for a place to camp along the road. My sweater and trousers were black and I was going on and off the shoulder of the road to avoid occasional oncoming traffic. A small silver car passed me going my way and stopped one hundred yards ahead. It paused like an animal that waits to inspect something strange in its environment from a safe distance, then came towards me in reverse. I watched this while blandly standing still, waiting to see what would happen. The car went a little behind me then caught up to me again. The window rolled down and a woman with silver hair and two children asked me if I was alright.

"I'm fine, I'm just looking for a place to camp."

"It's all private here, you have to *ask* the farmers."

"I'm sure it will be O.K."

"You don't look O.K. What are you doing out now? What will you do?"

"Go to sleep soon I hope."

It was nice to have company. I barely spoke a word all day. She turned off her engine.

"Will you come with us? You seem to be alright. We live two miles from here. Would that upset your plans?"

What plans?

"No! That would be great. Generous."

"Get in then. Kids move over. An American is coming with us."

I got in and she started apologizing for the interruption.

"Our house is nothing fancy I'm afraid, but you're welcome to come in. My husband won't mind, he knows about travelers. Look! It's starting to rain. You can't camp out."

We went off the asphalt onto a bumpy dirt track.

"Don't worry about the bumps, we won't be on the road long. It's good to be out of the way though. We own a small house on what used to be part of a large farm. Lots of crofters lived in this area. Now some of them are being divided up. When you see our house it looks long and large, but the house part of it is actually four rooms. Most of it is barn."

It was raining hard now and the temperature dropped. At the house we got out and walked through the wet grass to the door. I wondered what her husband would really think.

"What's your name? I have to tell my family your name! This is silly." She giggled.

Her husband looked serious but welcomed me and said I couldn't camp out. I would have to sleep in the house. We went upstairs to a room filled with good-natured clutter, toys and computers. I clunked my gear in a corner and put on a dry sweater.

"Robert, would you like some tea? Are you hungry at all?"

"Tea would be fine. I'm cold."

I sat down with her husband who told me he was a wood crafter and brought out a photo book to show samples of his work.

"How can you make a living doing this? It's so rural here," I asked.

"I go to Dundee, Perth and Aberdeen. My things sell there alright."

The children came in and imitated my accent.

"Ang, ang, ang," they said through their noses.

"Shoo you children. He's our guest." Mary entered with a tray of tea. She bent over to fix our cups and settled into a wingback chair to give us her attention. As she got organized I realized I had been waiting for her to return. Her eccentric good will warmed the room.

"Robert, how long have you been here? A long time?"

"No, I just started. I'm getting to know the country. Have you been here long?"

"Fourteen years."

"Are the people different when you go from area to area? You know, are there regionalisms in Scotland?"

"A little. The people here aren't very friendly. We are still regarded as English newcomers. Even after fourteen years."

I told her about my uneventful visit to the pub in Drumlithie.

"We used to go there," said Mary, "It was owned by a different family. They were strange. He was a *dour* man, *dour*. Do you know? And his wife sometimes helped him serve. I don't think they were suited to the business. When they made you a drink, especially the wife, it was as if they didn't want you to have it; it was like they didn't want to pass it to you or let it go. They would pour it and begrudgingly release it to you. She didn't like taking her fingers from around the glass. They were in the wrong business I think. To own a pub you have to like a frolic and gayness. They didn't."

"The husband used to drink too much," added Douglas, "Once some kids went in and he was passed out behind the bar. The Mrs. found the children serving themselves sodas from the tap. Over the body of the man as he lay there."

"The new owners are a little better suited to it, but we were never really accepted here," Mary continued, "I think they don't like outsiders. We rarely go there."

"What was this area like in the past, when it was one big farm?"

"It was organized and the core people of the town didn't change much. The room we're sitting in, for instance, was filled with beds for the hired workers. The people worked for food, lodging and a small wage."

"Up until the nineteen thirties farmers would have annual meetings where men who needed jobs would go and show themselves to the land owners. The workers would put tickets in their hats to show they were available for a period of indenture for wages," explained Douglas.

"It sounds a little like slavery."

"Not so bad, but feudal in nature. The landowners had lots of advantages. In the west they had the Highland 'Clearances' which were very cruel. The landowners decided that sheep were worth more than agricultural products, so they ended the farming and threw out the tenant farmers and laborers. This was in the early part of the last century. The people were thrown off with nowhere to go. Entire villages of people went to North America then. It was bitter. The memory is part of Scottish identity."

Douglas paused, "Now people are moving to the east. North Sea oil is drawing people here. We hope our house will go up in value."

"Robert, are you sure you're not hungry?" offered Mary.

"No thanks, I hope I'm not keeping you awake."

"Oh no, we need at least three cups of tea to go to bed. I'll go fetch some more."

When she came back she brought an album with her and showed me pictures of the area. Mary was trained as a teacher for disabled children and had even spent time teaching in Botswana. From the photos it looked like they were thoughtful hippies in the past. Mary was now teaching Kindergarten at a local Steiner school.

"Here is where our neighbors live. They are very unfriendly. And here is a photo of the grounds. The original farm was quite large. You can't see the end of it."

The tray was removed and Mary made a mattress for me.

"I hope it's all right?"

I looked at the rain spattering the windows. Of course it was alright. We said goodnight and turned out the lights.

In the middle of the night someone put an extra blanket on me.

———————

I woke up to a sad drizzle tapping the roof and windows. Mary sat in the kitchen and looked out the window, illuminated by the grey light.

"Can I get you breakfast, Robert? Tea?"

We had tea and she showed me alternative routes to get back on the main road.

"There's a walk-path you can take to get to the road quickly, but you'd better not do it."

"Why?"

"It goes by our neighbors'. I told you a little about them last night."

"They are unfriendly," I repeated.

"Needlessly so. When they moved in they wouldn't let us use the path anymore. We had to go three quarters of a mile out of our way if we wanted to walk to the road. We introduced ourselves and told them about the path, then asked if they minded if we continued to use it. They said no."

Mary made a minor look of chagrin.

"Later they called and told us that our children had stolen heather out of their garden. They had no proof and my children respect others' property. Heather is important, it brings good luck they say. Feelings hardened on their part. It was unnecessary, but so." She paused and frowned over the disturbing memory. "I'll drive you if you like. Are you sure you don't want some eggs?"

Her story and the rain induced a reverie in me. I collected my thoughts and responded to her offer.

"No, tea is fine, and I don't mind the walk. It's good to see the area in daylight."

Mary sipped her tea and looked distracted as she sat in the rocker. I shuffled my pack around and sank a bit when I opened the door. It was going to be wet for awhile. Mary waved as I left and followed the dirt path to the small main road.

I followed curving roads and stone fences until the afternoon when I reached Edzell and stopped for a meal in a place out of the chilly wind. The town of Edzell is organized around the main street. It is so direct and without imagination, I felt like chastising them for being so lazy. There were lots of accommodations for summer visitors to the site of an old castle nearby. I stopped in a small tea room, which had a dining area and a separate entrance for a fish and chips take-out trade. Out of politeness I didn't sit at the larger empty tables and chose a small table in an alcove section of the dining room directly behind another table for two. Almost immediately the place filled up with customers who wanted their evening meal. I asked the waitress for a salad plate and she came back with my beverage and what looked like a mayonnaise frenzy. There were pasta spirals in mayonnaise, ham and pickle in mayonnaise, potatoes and onions in mayonnaise and a portion of grated cheese with a fermenting pineapple ring on top. I could hear it make a little foaming noise. A small green salad accompanied it which was dressed with something sweet that tasted like it was made from oil out of the deep fryer.

I sent back the pineapple ring and the black haired matron froze a look at me across the restaurant as she listened to the waitress explain my dissatisfaction. I looked at her for a second and turned my attention back to my meal. If I didn't eat fast the whole thing would slide off my plate, which looked like a food version of an ecological disaster. My environment had been spoiled by an errant mayonnaise slick.

Midway through my grated cheese, a party of two sat at the table behind me. The chair directly opposite my back collided with my own. I pulled in to allow the woman to sit down and when we were settled, my abdomen was touching the table edge. I tried to move the table but it was bound to the floor. My hands and arms were thrust past my plate and I had to eat as if I was buttoning my shirt, reaching in towards myself. I tried sitting sideways, which worked better, but I was ear to hair with my bouffanted neighbor who said nothing. I continued to eat with this added, involuntary intimacy while little curls of pasta kept falling off my fork, which had to travel a longer distance from plate to mouth in my new position. Quickly, the area around me looked like an infant had dined there. The owner snuck mournful glances at me, which seemed to lament the fact that the foreign homeless had found rural Scotland.

After three cups of tea, for each of which I was charged, I decided to go before my clothes were soaked with the unctuousness of my skin. If I moved, perhaps I could do a metabolic dodge and use up the mayonnaise before it ruined my down coat. I went out to the main road and walked past the stern set of shops set in a line. By dark (10:30), I wanted to be in Brigend and camp. It looked about seven kilometers away.

Chapter Three

Apres loo cocktails and eccentrics

I passed the ruins of what must have been a huge castle and stopped to stare at a nearby garden. It had a carefully chosen variety of distinctive plants, shrubs, trees, flowers, and lawn and was tidily organized in a rectangle with paths leading through it. As I reached a small graveyard the sky lightened and stopped drizzling. I went along in silence for about two hours through purple-capped hills until it started to rain hard. I hid under a small pine forest until the worst had passed and then continued on the cold, wet road.

At nine O'clock, I came upon a town marked on the map as Balfield. It was four houses. As I stood there it rained a soaking mist and two children stared out the window of their house at me. I leaned my pack against my leg and stared at my map as it absorbed water. The children screamed to get my attention and ducked under the window when I looked over. I really wanted to be inside their house. It was dusk and looked warm there. I walked over and tapped on the window. It louvered open and an older girl appeared whom I asked for instructions to Brigend. She reached through the window and pointed on my map. She said go fifteen minutes down the path and you'll find it. It was getting steeper but I walked on and passed a small settlement whose most prominent feature was a small trailer park. A half-mile past the park was an array of stone homes, one of which advertised a Bed and Breakfast from a sign hung in the front yard. It was absolutely dark now. When I knocked on the door, nothing happened. I looked at the empty milk bottles waiting for collection and longed for domesticity. I waited a little longer then walked back to the trailer park I had passed earlier. The sky turned brown and rained short water strings through the air. I would have been impressed with the nuances and variety of precipitation that kept being displayed, if I had not been seriously sleepy.

At the trailer park I called to some people who were playing cards inside. They looked dry as they sat in front of the large picture window at the trailer rear.

"Can I camp here?" I called through the window. "Is there and empty trailer for a night? Anything?"

"Don't know, we're not the office." The voice was muffled by the plate glass. It sounded like we were speaking underwater.

"Sorry."

"The owner is a farmer five minutes from here, go around the bend to the second farm on the left." I watched the silhouette move in time with the barely audible words. His arm was black against the gold light of the lamp inside. The place had the warm, self-contained look of a Jack-O- Lantern.

I went back in the direction I came from and ascended a hill. The farm was at least a mile away and there were several in this vicinity on the left. The homes all were set about one half mile from the road on long driveways. I would have had to walk a mile and a half to get a door slammed in my face for knocking at this hour so I went back to the park and looked around. It was eleven thirty and hard to see in front of me. I looked around again and set up my tent in the drizzle. Then I put down my ground cloth and went to sleep.

At two thirty A.M. I woke up because my stomach was cold. It was cold because my sleeping bag was soaked to my waist. The tent had leaked. I didn't want to move. I lay there in half consciousness for fifteen minutes wondering if this would go away. If I wiggled my feet I could hear sloshing, as if they were in a shallow pool. I sat up to discover they were. So was my pack. The entire perimeter of the tent interior was like a moat. I was exhausted and couldn't think clearly. I didn't want to know about this worst-case scenario which was happening to me. I felt for my gear and found a yard square high spot on the tent floor that was dry. After gathering my things around me like children, I sat cross-legged in the upper half of my sleeping bag. For forty-five minutes I sat in a wet haze and tried to sleep. I let my head hang, then tried resting it in my palms. A small reclining wall I made out of my stuff collapsed into the little moat when I leaned on it. Exhaustion ate at me but I got out of the tent and looked at it. It looked fine. My shoes made squishing noises as I walked around it. Nothing could be done. This is what it must feel like to be retarded, I thought. I had no idea what I should do next and I couldn't imagine any possibilities. My thoughts came in short disconnected flashes as it continued to rain on me.

The dark outline of a utility building was nearby. I assumed it was storage for the park and I took wet steps towards it. There were no lights and I decided to break in if I could. I stumbled on a concrete step and banged into an aluminum wall that thundered when I hit it. After I recovered my balance, I waited for every light to come on and braced for a drove of bathrobed families carrying torches to burn me out. It remained silent. I looked up to discover I was standing in front of a sign that said "Ladies"

"That's me," I thought. I pushed the door a little and it opened. Oh, haven of three toilets and a special wastebasket for sanitary napkins! I accept! I ran out as well as I could and dragged my pack and sleeping bag inside. Then I went out, took down the tent, and brought it into the ladies room. The toilet looked like a staging area for an expedition. It was out of Samuel Beckett.

"Men, the project will operate out of our nerve center, the ladies' room."

I squeezed a quart and a half of water from my sleeping bag and hung it on the pegs where the ladies put their shower caps to dry. The tent was spread over the frames of three toilet stalls and my clothes hung on the toilet doors, which swung open. It would be hard to escape if someone came in. I moved from toe to toe in nervousness. Oh well, they'd understand. I would tell them I was lost, or I got off at the wrong train station. Maybe if I just stood naked and chewed on my boot I wouldn't have to answer any questions.

Next to the toilets was a shower stall. When I figured out the eccentric design of the operating switches, a stream of hot water came out. I took this to be proof that God had noticed me and got in. After forty minutes in the shower, I dried off with yards of toilet paper. I picked off the little paper flecks that stuck to my skin, dressed in my damp clothes, and sat on a toilet lid in the dark. My thoughts had been running at an incredible pace and as I sat there I wondered what's the rush? Calm down, it's nice here. My watch said four A.M..

The only comfortable position in the narrow stall was one in which my back was slumped against the water closet so that my shoes could reach the closed stall door and rest with my soles flat against it supported by friction. At five thirty, my feet fell from the door and startled me from my half sleep. The garlands of camping equipment were dry enough to be packed and I cleared out before anyone could charge me for the shower.

I wanted coffee and rafts of toast with eggs. A mile up the road the B and B was still closed. I walked two more miles to Brigend, which was four houses. A car came by and I asked the driver where there was a place to stop.

"There are none. You'll have to go to Careston seven miles away."

I didn't want to go anymore but I went over the steep, long hill and continued for five more miles until I came to the tiny Careston intersection where there was a house and a post office. The sun came out and my sweater started to steam. I saw nowhere to stop here, so I went three more miles to the nearest town on the map, where I had my hair cut by a young girl who hated to speak, then a bowl of chicken potato soup in a pub. The waitress asked if I had come a long way. I told her what had happened and she laughed.

"Ha, you were a quarter mile from a little restaurant in Careston. You just had to go down the hill from where you started towards here. It's near the big highway. Ho, Ho." I pulled my soup closer for solace and acted as if I didn't want to talk about it any more. After an hour I left the hilly, small labyrinth of Brechin and walked out towards my next stop, Memus.

At the Memus intersection was a severe stone church and an inn called The Drover's. A little further on was a campground and caravan park. I walked by the parking area towards the office and noticed the rectangular, economical shapes of the car trailers. They didn't have the swagger and scale of American models and seemed arrested and small. The dense green grass was trimmed and parking was done neatly despite the lack of designated and numbered lots. The guests were self regulating and use of the area was made without the over-imposition of form. The owner helped me to a place where it was dry and protected from the wind. I bought some Venison chops and cooked them on a borrowed grill, then lay down for my first undisturbed sleep in thirty hours.

I woke up with a start. I didn't know where I was and why I had the taste of animal fat in my mouth. I stared through the green light in my tent and remembered that I was camping and walking through Scotland. I wanted alcohol and company. My disorientation stayed with me as I put on my sweater and down coat and walked shakily past a small stream in the brisk clear evening towards the "Drover's". In the course of the quarter mile walk to the Inn the sky changed from mostly grey, to grey and white, to grey and bright yellow with sneaks of blue and was like a film presentation of accelerated time.

The Drover's had a foyer entrance and small panelled walkway that brought me to the division between the bar and dining room. I chose right to the lounge and sat next to a large window. Behind the six foot bar was a tight selection of bottles with clear portion dispensers designed to give the purchaser confidence he is getting what he paid for. The bar took up one quarter of the area in the small square room, which could seat sixteen people in close proximity. The ceiling was low and square and the spot lighting created orange and brown comfort zones as it illuminated the dark wood bar and tables. People gradually came in for bar suppers and drinks and the spareness of the place allowed for the human presence to prevail over the architectural scheme. My whiskey came and I sipped it greedily, then ordered another with coffee. Two tables filled with diners on either side of my place surrounded me with the bulk of sweaters and mumbling conversation. It was intimate and private at the same time. The Scotch and company was inducing a gentle euphoria.

"Where are you from?"

The man next to me wanted to talk. He looked about fifty and had all his hair. His face was worn a bit but handsome and roguish. His pretty wife smiled in my direction and exposed her buck teeth. The coarse hairs on his sweater rustled as he turned towards me for a conversation.

"The States," I answered.

"We were thinking Italy or maybe France."

"No, L.A.."

"I want a drink," he looked to his wife, "Do we have any money?" She took out some coins.

"What do you think of it here?"

"It's interesting, but I'm still new. I'm figuring things out. Where are you from?"

"We live here, but I'm really Irish."

"Oh, are they different from the Scots?"

"*No!*" he said and shook his head, "We're the same thing, all Celts. *Exactly* the same."

"You mean all Celts are the same?"

He nodded up and down, "Yes!"

"You don't look like an American."

"I am, born in Detroit."

"What's that like?"

"It used to be nice, but race problems and the big industries have spoiled it."

"Do Americans have pubs?"

"Not really. There are some neighborhood bars, but we aren't as sociable a people. Very individualistic and find human proximity uncomfortable. It can be raw in my country. We have places to drink but they don't have the living room ambience and fellowship of Scots' pubs. Our idea of a pub is different."

"I've never been there." He paused and thought for a moment.

"Suppose you're out of work there, then what?"

"Then nothing. You can get some benefits based on your last year's earnings, but when those run out, that's it."

"That's too hard. Here we have a dole and housing assistance for as long as you need."

He turned to his wife:

"Did you hear that, they let their own people suffer?"

He turned back to me abruptly.

"Do you want a drink? Do we have any money?" he asked wife. She took out some coins.

"What do you want?"

My Scotch came and he told me his name was Colin.

"Why are you so strange looking; dark?"

"Maybe because I'm Jewish."

He opened his mouth a little and leaned closer.

"Fascinating."

"Really? Why?"

"Don't you see man, you're separate from us by an entire continent. We're up here in the stones and wet where Celts should be, across the channel are the Europeans, then there are the Turks, Arabs and Jews. You're quite exotic. I mean nothing by it, mind you."

"I'm hardly a Jew at all anymore."

"It's O.K., I said. You're alright. In an odd way we have something in common."

"What?"

"Do you want to come home with us and sleep by our hearth? It's better than outside."

"I'm all set up, and it's dark." I really wanted to go to his house, but I couldn't raise the energy to take down my tent and move.

"What do we have in common?"

"It's the Druidic idea that God is inside you. Immanence."

"Jews don't believe that."

"Let me finish. With Immanence, you don't need a priest like the Roman Catholics. You go directly to God. Jews have that don't they? A personal relationship to God? You know, I mean directly to God. I know this. I read about it. And here you are wandering about. The wandering Jew. Ho! Do you want another drink? Have we any money? This is *in*teresting."

His wife went to her purse again. A boy with them asked me why I became a Jew. I explained that I was born into it.

"What about this chosen business," Colin interjected, "You're not better than us. What does it mean?"

"We had a deal, God gets us out of Egypt and we become his representatives for the purpose of showing His true identity and moral thought."

"Fascinating, are you coming with us?"

I wanted to badly. I was too settled. The bell rang for last drinks.

"I don't have the energy to move."

"Well, alright, how much is he charging you there?"

"I don't know."

"Don't pay it, get up early and leave. It'll be O.K.."

"I couldn't do that."

"It's O.K.. I know him. Where are you going next?"

"London, for a couple of days, for work."

"Sit in the toilet on the train, it will save you fifty pounds."

His wife and I laughed.

"One more thing, is it really as violent as they say in America? I saw your city burning on the television. I read where there are four hundred murders a year in your big cities. Each."

"Yes, it's true."

"Here there are almost none. If you read the local papers, which I admit are small, you will find that the police are asking for the thief of a bicycle to please return it to its rightful owner. That's what we have."

"You're not as diverse a people in Scotland."

"Last chance. We're leaving."

"Thanks, better not, bye."

Chapter Four

Celtic Glow

The flaps of my tent rapped against the tight nylon walls and woke me. It was a clear and gentle, breezy morning. At the Drover's I had some coffee and planned a route for the Lake of Lintrathen. As I arranged my gear outside, a man stood next to his huge Mercedes and cooed to an Airedale puppy,

"Hello darling, sweet thing, yes, you're a love."

A couple of other men stood around looking at the young dog. No one seemed embarrassed by the language he used and the man continued to scratch and cuddle it.

After a mile the landscape became abruptly wooded with more ups and downs. At the crossing of the south Esk river was a huge gate with a church next to it. On the other side of the gate was a large area with tended lawns that looked like it was part of an estate. There was no one there so I walked in and went down towards the river to look at it. Water rights in Scotland are all private and this portion had no fence around it. The only security was probably the large iron gate which was open. I felt I was on private property but I didn't care. I was going to wait until I was asked to leave. The conception of this place was foreign to me. All this nature was so tended and organized.

As I stood there near the bank looking for trout, a man on horseback came along the road inside the gate and stopped. We stared at each other and I walked towards him. As he waited for my approach, he tweaked a horsehair whip about his head to chase the flies. His presence was not American. He looked about fifty-five and wore high leather boots and riding pants. The crown of his head swept back from the plane of his face, led by the perfect line of his nose. The proportions were perfectly balanced. He was a little curious, but spoke with the calmness of someone who felt he would determine the outcome of whatever the conversation brought.

"Is this private property?" I asked.

"Yes, but it's alright." His tone played down the importance of his ownership.

"There was no one at the gate, so I walked in."

He swatted flies as he spoke and his horse shifted.

"No, it's fine, have a look around. Where are you from?"

I told him. He looked entertained and smiled. It was a soft expression. His manner had warmth.

"The grounds are big, go down the road if you like. Our home is over there." He pointed with his whip away from the entrance.

"Thanks."

"Bye."

He turned his horse and sauntered off. Local nobility I thought. I noticed his accent was English and wondered what he did for a living. What a contrast he was to the American image of powerful men who made their fortunes in the nineteenth century. Cigar chomping tough guys who made something from nothing in the frontier. I wondered if the man I had just met had ever called anyone a "son of a bitch."

The terrain became steeper and at the top of the hill before the lake. I could see the humps of the surrounding loaf-like hills. An old man in black and a blond boy came towards me from the opposite direction. They had a black dog on a long leash whose spontaneity was in contrast to the slow and deliberate movements of the man, who looked about eighty-five. He put himself on the grass to rest, where he made an angular, delicate figure.

The boy stood and smiled while the dog jumped all over me. His accent was hard to understand.

"Where are you heading?"

"To lake Lintrathen."

"Aye, you'll find nowhere to stay there."

"I'm camping, but isn't there a hotel down the way?"

"There is but it's far too duff for the likes of you."

"What is duff?"

"Gentlemen and ladies with proper clothes."

His manner was crusty and matter of fact. He was helping me and kept stopping to think before speaking. We had a big pause.

"You can go down to the village," he paused and looked up, "You can go further to a place with tables, but it's only coffee."

I took off my pack. The sun was deep yellow and wisps of clouds were stretched about the blue sky. We all rested together. The boy's complexion was white and his hair was yellow with a white cast. His voice had no corners. It was impossibly obliging without effort. The man took my map and tapped it with his two fingers together.

"Here is where you go," he pointed, "You can walk there and see if you like it. You can go further if you want. We'll be going now."

The boy helped him up and the old man righted himself with his walking stick. The boy had no guile at all. I said thanks and goodbye and he waved with soft goodwill.

Two miles further I stood at a small intersection with houses. I pulled out my map and stood there. There was no place to camp and nothing to eat. A man pulled out of his driveway and stopped. His dog made a racket in the back seat and snarled at me.

"You're lost," he smiled.

"Not really, just looking for a place to eat. An elderly man said I could find something here. This is the village isn't it?"

"He wasn't as old as me was he?" he chuckled.

"*Much* older, between eighty and ninety."

"Wait here a second, don't worry about the dog. Ginger, shut up! She wouldn't hurt anything."

He smiled fondly at her as saliva flew from her mouth while she raged. At his house he tapped on the window, His wife appeared and he gestured as they spoke through the opening. He walked back smiling.

"You can stay here if you like," and pointed with his arm towards the front yard. His house looked oddly suburban in this neighborhood of stone.

"I need a place to wash too. I don't think it would work. You're very generous though. "I waited for him to offer to use his bathroom. We stood there kind of fumbling and smiling. His dog got out of the car and snarled at me.

"Don't worry about old Ginger." It was hard not to.

"So you're going on are you?"

"I'd better. I was told there is a place for coffee nearby, could you give me directions?"

He gave me instructions which I immediately forgot, and went on. The lake was surprisingly empty. It was a clear mid-summer evening and only three boats were on it. A couple was parked in their car and eating while they stared out at the shore. I walked past the gates of a fishing authority and after four miles entered the driveway to the small restaurant I wanted. A dog ran towards me at full speed, barking and showing its teeth which were at testicle level. A man in blue jeans torn at the knees ran after it.

"Get back here."

I screamed at the dog as it came towards me. Four people moved to the center of the drive to see why I was shouting like an animal and watch the dog approach my genitals. A black-haired lady apologized for the dog.

"He's never like that, except rarely."

The men stood around and looked at me. They wondered what I was going to do next after cursing the dog. They were a motley crew. One had bushy hair and a ragged shirt. The owner had huge forearms and the third had the knees of his jeans out. They looked raw as they fiddled with a tractor part and tried to fix it with the point of a dart. I wondered if they were mad at me for yelling at their dog. The man with the ripped jeans kept telling the dog to be quiet and held it as it strained against its collar.

"You were brave to face our dog like that," the woman said.

"It was mostly fear, I get angry when I'm afraid. Are you open?"

"'Fraid not. Closed at five thirty." It was now eight O'clock.

"Can I pitch a tent here? I've come a long way."

"You're aggressive," she laughed, "I thought you might be Canadian but it must be America. I guess you can, come 'round to the back."

I followed her around the house to the rear which had short grass like a golf course. The men went back to fixing machinery in the stone barn. The lawn looked comfortable. I went up and down under the wires for the outdoor clothes drying.

"How much do you charge?"

"No, nothing, just buy coffee and scones in the morning. Put your tent anywhere. Do you want to come in?"

"Sure."

They had a large country kitchen. An older grandmother was putting raspberry preserves in jars and greeted me. There was a large urn for coffee and rich jam tarts left over from the coffee shop. The grandmother poured coffee and invited me to sit with them in the parlor where her daughter, the owner, was conducting an argument with her ten year old about a bath. It was odd to hear them argue. The girl was insubordinate and assumed an authority and aggressiveness beyond her age. Her mother did-n't press her. I expected a more stern response.

"Come sit down. This is Hugh, my grandson."

She pronounced Hugh with a gravelly end. Finally the arguments stopped. The daughter avoided a bath by browbeating her mother. I felt she had gotten away with murder. Her mother settled into a chair.

"Do you want another jam tart?" Generosity was easy for her.

"No thanks."

"Have a bath then, there's lots of hot water now that my daughter's gone."

I walked down the corridor to the bath. It was an old farmhouse which was starting to settle. The floors were a little uneven. The longer I stayed inside, the more they offered me. I wiggled my toes in the warm water and wondered what they would give me next. The tub must have been six and a half feet long. As I soaked, I looked at the precise, old slat clapboards on the wall. The design of the house was no-nonsense but comfortable. We sat in the parlor and turned on the T.V.. The Olympics were on, and in between events the women asked me about America. The husband came in and settled into his chair, distracted by the boxing match between an Irishman and a Thai. He was tired and his curly hair was a little unkempt from the day's operation of the sheep farm he ran. His worked hands and strong forearms clutched the rests on his chair. He looked like a belligerent person at ease. I was worried that he didn't want his wife's generosity to interfere with his life.

"The Thai looks good, but the Irishman is ahead in points I think," I looked over sheepishly.

He observed me with heavy lidded eyes and a slack mouth.

"Aye, the Irish can fight."

No hostility. I relaxed a bit.

"Someone told me all Gaelics are alike, is that true? The Irish have a reputation for fighting."

"It is true," he hesitated, "Basically we're all alike. Scots don't like to fight as much." He raised his brow, "Irish are a little wicked."

He was being obliging through his haze of fatigue. His wife came in with a variety of sweets and a huge plate of sandwiches.

"Go ahead, more coffee? You're our guest."

I thanked her and tried her husband a little more.

"I rarely see lamb in the groceries or restaurants. Who buys your products? Is the money just in wool?"

He looked over at me and raised his brow without opening his eyes further. It was a bored look, but wasn't directed at me. It was non-specific. He was bored with his own life.

"Well, theoretically, you're supposed to make money at this." He thrust his hands in his pockets and sank in his chair, "But the Scots don't buy it. We get a subsidy for each head, but we're not a mutton- eatin'-country. French buy it when their trucks aren't blockading the roads."

We turned our attention back to the boxing.

"How have you found the Scots?" His wife asked me.

"So far everyone has been helpful."

"Around here, people are polite, even the Lord of Cortachy will say hello in the shop and chat a bit."

"Who is that? I think I met him!"

"He lives in a great estate in Cortachy."

"I was there! Today! I saw him on his horse."

"Yes, he'll take his exercise on a horse."

"How does he make his living, I mean what does he do all day?"

"Well, he gets appointed to lots of directors' boards, and he administers his estates and ground rents. He is also a true member of the aristocracy, a Chamberlain to the Queen."

"What is a Chamberlain?"

"Well, it's a person who does arranging for the Queen's receptions and social functions. He's like the Queen's caterer."

"Royalty, and I met him. He was kind of funny and polite."

"Not royalty, aristocracy. Yes, he'll talk to you. Things aren't like in the old days. More and more people are buying their land. It used to be that you could only own the house and the Lord owned the land. You had to pay rent for the ground under your house. Now people can buy the land too. Feudal, you know. Things are changing. More equal."

I decided to go to the tent.

"Thanks for the hospitality."

"No, don't mention it, there will be a girl in the shop in the morning, She'll fix you up. I have to leave until eleven in the morning."

"I can do business with your husband if you aren't here."

"No, there's no charge. Goodnight."

In the tent I prepared for sleep. Over the tent floor I put a ground cloth and my rain coat. Before getting into my inadequate sleeping bag, I put on my down coat. The bag was an old one borrowed from an English friend and it was an eccentric design. It was big enough for one body, but you couldn't roll over in it. You had to roll over with the entire bag following you like a wool carapace. In addition, I was awakened by the cold every night. And there was never a frost. The bag was good if you wore a coat and the temperature remained above fifty-five degrees F. I thought of filling it full of lamb shit and mailing it back to my friend, but the freight was too high. In the morning I was woken up by the sounds of sheep running back and forth.

"Come on, bring 'em in."

I looked out the tent and saw my host following a herd with the same bored look on his face as last night, while giving instructions to his dog. The dog chased the sheep according to his different calls and whistles. I watched to make sure this wasn't an accident. The dog changed its behavior with each different command and eagerly chased the sheep around. In the coffee shop, their fourteen-year-old daughter came in from the back lawn, put on her shoes and ran to serve me when she saw me walk in the dining room. She was unprofessional and homey. The shop was typically Scottish with pine tables set in a stone room with white square window frames. It was a combination of severity and comfort zones with linen runners on the tables and soft light from outside. At eleven thirty, I walked out and passed my hostess as she came up the drive.

"An early start is it?" She laughed.

Chapter Five

Tax the land and the fish

I trudged on to Glenisla and treated myself to lunch in the local hotel. The terrain was getting steeper and I wanted protein. Pickled Orkney herrings sounded fleshy, so I ordered them. The pickle was disappointingly sweet and I picked at them slowly while I observed the middle aged and elderly tourists gently consume their lunches. The puffy lipped waitress stood by my table and said nothing. She wore black tights and had a natural, cheery rudeness. If something distracted her, she would immediately end whatever conversation she was having to tend to the new stimulus. I had to wait through three interruptions to give her my order. She was stupid and happy. After I ate, I sat at the bar and asked her about the area. She was from Dundee and said it had problems.

"Some unemployment, the people get mean sometimes. I have a girlfriend whose boyfriend head-butts her. He's a big bloke. Would scare the likes of most men. A bikey too. Problems with drugs are moving in."

"Heroin?"

"No, not in this little place, but Kirriemuir is the biggest drug town in the area."

I couldn't believe it. I had stopped in Kirriemuir to go shopping one afternoon. It was incredibly cute. The main streets ran through it in a variety of angles. The town center was almost medieval with crescents of stone and wood store fronts following the jumbled intersections of the main square. It was surrounded by hills in the north and trickled out downhill in a small road heading south. As I walked out, old ladies walking arm in arm had smiled at me and spoke of the sunshine.

"I am surprised to hear it."

"Don't be, around Aberdeen it's good, other places can be hard. Money you know."

"What kind of drugs?"

"I couldn't say, marijuana for sure though."

She broke off our conversation as if I wasn't there to talk to a girl who entered from the kitchen.

I smoked a bit and walked out. It became overcast and started to rain at Brewland's Bridge, so I stood in the vestibule of a hotel and watched. For a while, it was slippery and grey. The sky lightened and became a sober steel color. I walked up a long, desolate hill to an unmarked lake on the map. At the east end, it was primitive and private. I put down my pack and bounded over the heather and grassy clumps to look at the shore. Egrets were skimming the surface and a trout jumped towards the center. I ran back to get my pack and fishing line. I didn't have a permit for the lake, but it could wait. Wild trout in an undiscovered lake couldn't be missed. I walked further along to the west where the water was deeper and I could get a better cast. I half ran across the uneven terrain and fumbled with my hooks and bait. I couldn't wait and just as I reached the rocky point from where I was going to end the lives of many fish in illicit privacy, I came upon seventeen people with binoculars watching the egrets. I stuffed my fishing gear behind my back and grinned at the unexpected group of tourists who were bird watching. I heard another trout jump and felt like a child visiting relatives who bore him. I didn't want to wait another minute, I wanted to get back to my house and the dirty magazine hidden in my room.

The sky broke up and white light filtered through the stack of clouds overhead. Two more fish jumped. The piles of people on their car hoods didn't budge. Some of them looked at the birds through the windows of their cars. What a dispassionate approach to nature. Bird watching from the road with binoculars. Overcivilized. It's like watching someone else eat or have sex. I wanted to tell them, "People, get out there, catch fish, sleep on the ground, *do* something." I ran downhill to see if there was a spot to cast away from the sight of the crowd. At the entrance to a road at the extreme western end of the lake a sign said, "No fishing, *Private.*" A large trout broke the surface near me. The bird watchers were on a high bluff from where the whole lake was visible. I stared for a while at the thick currents made by the fish rises and felt that connection between myself and the life in the lake. I wanted to feel a fish on my line. I watched the water for a half hour and looked back up at the birdwatchers. They were having their effete bird watching at the expense of my poaching. I dug at the ground with my toe and looked at the teeming life breaking the surface of the lake until my anguish forced me to leave.

I bitterly made my way down the hill. This place was too domesticated. Private ponds and streams. Bird watching. Nature limited to an observable phenomenon. Scotland looked like the back yard for the English. Under these conditions, it is a duty to steal fish just to maintain a standard of spirit. Two miles down the main road a fisherman and his small boys casted in the river. I watched silently for a while until the man looked up at me.

"Anything?" I asked.

"Not now, salmon are starting to come up the river though."

"Hi!" called his son in a happy non-sequitor.

"What are you using?" I asked.

"Hello!" called the boy again.

"Hi," I answered. The brothers smiled at each other.

"We use flies or worms. Whatever works, and nothing is working now."

"Hello!" called the younger boy and looked at his brother.

"He's American, I heard him say."

"Stop interrupting, he's trying to talk." said the Dad.

"Hi! Hello!" they chimed, "We want to hear him talk."

Their father smiled and looked at the stream.

"Is there a place to camp here?" I asked.

"We like to camp," said the older boy.

"Down one mile and to the left, you'll find a grounds and a hotel. Just past Blacklunans."

"Bye!" screamed the boys.

The sun came out and the evening became grey and gold. At the hotel the lounge was empty. In the silent bar, two girls spoke privately. They were dressed provocatively and I wondered where they were going to meet boys. It was quiet in the area. I ordered a light meal and went back to the parlor to watch a Scottish girl on T.V. competing in the ten thousand meter race. The bar man wandered in with my food and watched the competition. Within five minutes the rest of the hotel staff, about four older women in their fifties and sixties, were in the parlor watching. They sat in a pile on the couch and made a little Caledonian cheering section in their part of the room. For a while, the Scottish girl held the lead and the ladies bounced up and down and shook bulky arms and chins. She couldn't hold the lead but the women jostled each other in good nature and made jokes abut the Muslim runners in T-shirts. Some adolescent boys came in with French Fries and tidy sweaters. They giggled to themselves about the scanty outfits and glowed with good health and color. At the end of the race the women got up and trundled off to various stations of the hotel, laughing bawdily as they left the room. I walked out too and watched the mist settling on the dark hills to the west as I set up my tent.

In the morning, I walked about a mile south to an inn for morning coffee. The place wasn't open yet but the lady at the bar said it was alright to come in. A gaggle of Spanish tourists stood in the vestibule looking serious and confused. I walked past them to the open lounge area and sat until the manager came over and asked me what I liked. He was obliging considering the fact that they weren't open yet.

"Why don't you have an English breakfast?"

"O.K., what is it?"

"You know, bacon, eggs, toast."

"Mm."

"You look strange, you're not Spanish are you?"

"No, American."

"But you're different."

"I'm not part of a tourist group?"

"No, I'll bet your Jewish."

"How could you tell?"

"'Cause you look it! *Christ* what a question, it's obvious. Are you religious?"

"Not really."

He pulled a Star of David from under his shirt.

"I went to Sandhurst for military training. The officers who taught me were Jewish."

"Are you Jewish?"

"No, but I respected the men who ran the programs. I admired them, so I wear this."

"English traditions are quite good, why adopt a foreign connection?"

"I like them. I'm proud of the affiliation."

"Does religion matter up here? It doesn't seem to be a source of hostility."

"No, its not unless you are in Glasgow where the Protestant and Catholic schoolchildren used to spit at each other and that's mainly because the Catholics are Irish. People don't really care if you're Church of Scotland, Presbyterian, or Catholic. The only thing the Scots are *really* conscious of is the English."

"So the Scottish Presbyterianism isn't a big cultural influence?"

"Not as something that makes us intolerant of other people. What is or was big was our loss of power to the English after Culloden. The Western Scots bought it as a people and the tribal ways were finished. The clans fell apart, Cumberland butchered us, and the chiefs even went to the English side because that's where the power was. To maintain their fiefs and lands they had to cooperate with the English. Then there were the Clearances. People and politicians talk of separation, but as a country, we've had our chance. A long time ago. How could we separate? English need our water, our oil, and our space. You see the tourists at Inverness? We've become a green area for the English in their Bermuda shorts. Even some Arabs are buying here. We're outnumbered by about twelve times. What can we do? Nothing. It's funny though. Cumberland beat a bunch of starved clansmen and then punished them cruelly after. A hastily organized army was the only one he could beat. All the rest of his campaigns he lost. One of his defeats resulted in the disarming of thirty or forty thousand English soldiers and gave Hanover to the French. That's England for you. Indifferent to the spirit of our people. Think we come out of the hills smelling of peat to this day. Do you know they tried the poll tax on us before trying it on themselves? Laboratory mice we are. To them."

He got up, went to the kitchen, and returned with a stainless steel rack of toast and two snowy poached eggs next to pink bacon slices.

"What's the poll tax?" I asked as I grabbed toast with both hands.

"It's a tax for being alive."

"In America we saw pictures of the protests in London, but it wasn't clear what they were about. I mean, what the tax was for."

"If you were alive you paid it. It was a substitute for the rates."

"What are the rates?"

"Taxes on property. If you owned a lot you paid a lot."

"How are they different?"

"The poll tax taxed you just for being alive at an even rate. Every one paid the same. Regardless of income."

"That sounds equal."

"It was better with the rates. Then you paid according to your actual wealth. If you owned more because you made more, you paid a proportionate amount. A lot of people on fixed incomes were hurt by the poll tax. They couldn't plan for the amounts due."

"That's odd, in the states a lot of people on fixed incomes were hurt by progressive property taxes, The more your property was worth, the more it was taxed. In the New England area, about seven years ago, property values were rising at an average rate of three percent a month in some areas. That's huge. Older people on pensions found their property worth twice what it was a year or two before. The taxes went up and those who had old farmland with hundreds of acres had large bills. More than they could pay in some instances. Some had to sell."

"That's interesting, but the English could try it everywhere, not just in Scotland. It's discrimination it is. The tax was about three hundred pounds per head. But this is just complaining mind you. We'll stay part of the union. We have water, oil, and space. If we tried to leave, the English would fight. They'd have to."

"Makes sense."

"Enjoy your breakfast, do you need some warm toast? I've been talking 'til it got cold. You should talk to the owner. He's from America."

"I came to meet Scots."

A thin man, slightly bent, came out and sat at the small bar. He wore a narrow cowboy hat and spoke through his nose.

"Everybody have coffee heah?" He sounded like he was from Louisiana or Alabama. He raised the pot and looked around.

"We got a Yankee cup now, all you want."

He was funny and friendly.

"Where you from, buddy, sounds like the States?"

"That's me."

"Have some coffee!" He filled my cup. "It's good here in Scotland, isn't it?"

"Yes."

"I *know* it is. I own this business, lived in Loosiana, moved here. More coffee? Bottomless cup."

He visited with some people at another table. I could hear him across the room. His style was louder than the usual country inn, but the employees and regular customers at the bar liked him. He went outside and used a motorized weed cutter to trim the fences. It looked funny as the outdoor man of the Bayou used such a domesticating garden tool.

"You come back now," he said as I walked past, and tipped his cowboy hat up.

My nightly sleep interruptions were flagging my will. I was getting sick of walking and wanted to fool around. I did six miles and stopped at Kirkmichael where a relentless drizzle had started. The future was rain so I decided to put on my sponge best and loaf. At a tiny food market I asked for directions to a lodging. Three of the employees got quietly involved with helping me. At the gas and general store across the street a man offered to help me select fishing flies. I was attracting help and good will at a surprising rate.

I went to a Bed and Breakfast owned by a portly English couple off the main road. There were no other guests so the place was very still. The three of us sat quietly in the living room and had tea. Outside was a dreary gray and green visage, as I looked across the soccer field in front of the house. Despite the absence of guests, the husband wore a white laboratory coat. Its officiousness was in contrast to the absence of anything to do.

"Would you like an evening meal?"

"No thanks, I just want to rest."

He got up and came back with a clipboard and a printed sheet filled with columns and headings.

"Would you like porridge, cornflakes or meusli tomorrow?"

"Um, porridge please."

"Oat biscuits, toast, scones, or plain bread?"

"Toast please."

"Eggs fried, scrambled, coddled or poached?"

"Fried, easy over."

"Sausage or bacon?"

"Sausage."

"Coffee or tea?"

"Coffee."

"First or last?"

"In the middle."

He frowned and made notes on the board. I asked if I could use the kitchen to make a sandwich with things I had brought. They welcomed me to do so and I went in. Two little sausages were set out to thaw and a box of bread crusts was perched on top of the stove. Leftover oatmeal was formed into a spongy loaf and kept by the refrigerator. Their efforts at economy were serious and organized. I made my sandwich carefully so I didn't upset any arrangement they had and put utensils back at the angle and position in which I found them in their storage places. I went back into the living room and watched T.V. with the hosts. They welcomed my company with almost indiscernible, discreet appreciation.

"We like it here, down south was getting too crowded," said Mrs.

"Where were you from?"

"Manchester." The husband leaned forward and extinguished his cigarette. "How 'bout yourself?"

"U.S."

"Mmhm."

We turned our attention back to the T.V. and looked like a small row of theatre goers.

"I guess I'll be going to sleep now. Nite."

"Breakfast is at eight thirty. Shall I wake you a little before?"

"Yes, thanks."

He made a note on the clipboard.

In the morning, the dining room was set with precision and clarity. The owner came in with his lab coat and brought warm oatmeal, cream, butter, marmalade, and a rack of toast. Outside the picture window, it was white and raining. I ate the oatmeal, which seemed to be the food equivalent of Plutonium. It felt like it would be sufficient for days. My insides were lined with oat mucilage. The bowl was taken and replaced with a plate of eggs and mealy sausages. New toast was brought silently by the husband, who adopted a slightly distant air now that he was acting in an official capacity.

The coffee was brought in at the middle. I accidentally ate enough for thirty-six hours. A last appearance was made by the owner to ask if everything was alright. I felt he may have been standing by the door at attention throughout my breakfast. As I paid my bill, we chatted some more.

"Do you know of the old foot path to Pitlochry? It's supposed to go past old Crofts and a lake."

"We do, but it's wet today. You need real wet gear. The heather's high and its been raining for forty eight hours. You'd better stick to less rough country."

"It looks old and interesting."

"Yes, but you'd get soaked and without a detailed map you can't find your way. The paths are old and small. Here, take our card and tell people about us if you liked it."

"Are there lots of English people who run hospitality services in Scotland?"

"It's hard to find a hotel that isn't owned by the English. The B and Bs are a different situation. More local ownership."

He relaxed and took off his lab coat. I lifted my gear and walked through the foyer. It was a plain wet walk to Pitlochry.

I had a German girlfriend who showed me pictures of a trip she took to Rhodes. There were hundreds of tourists from the north in pastel shorts and orthopedic looking sandals walking up and down the roadways and staring at menus or sitting at crowded tables balancing beverage cups. When I arrived, Pitlochry was a damp version of this scene with boots and rain slickers substituted for Birkenstocks and summer clothes. It was like an outdoor grocery store with people milling up and down the asphalt aisle looking for a place to sit, consume, or buy a Scottish item. The spare Scottish Gemütlichkeit was displaced by the consumerism of the Northern European community with some Spaniards and Italians suspiciously present. Downtown Pitlochry had the feel of a starchy boutique.

Traditional plaid and bulky woolen goods were displayed in the shop windows. The locals clustered around the chip shops or Oriental take-outs while the visitors crowded the sidewalks, causing minor collisions when a group stopped to look at a restaurant display. I held my breath and leapt sideways out of the throng, which was carrying me up the street into the vestibule of a relatively large teashop. I was soaked.

My trousers were dark with wet and my walking shoes had split open. I looked like a transient beggar. My hat was dripping and clung to my skull like a thin helmet. The humidity drooped my sweater. I had to urinate. It was a resonant, sympathetic act of moisture on my bladder's part. A back table was empty so I went to it and sat down. The waiter stared at me as if my presence didn't project the normal expectations of customers and I felt I should reassure him that I wasn't going to ask him for money or steal the sugar and ketchup. I pulled my sweater away from my neck and thought, "Maybe I shouldn't do that." The waiter might worry about what would come out.

I got the menu and looked behind me for the specials on a blackboard. Haggis, potatoes, and parsnips sounded substantial. A polite young man came by and asked me for my choice of hot beverage. Was a bath included under this category? A large hot liquid? A suave French couple next to me sipped red wine and looked carelessly out the window. They didn't seem like their underwear was wet. Their pigskin gloves were rolled in tidy parcels in the middle of the table. I had to pee again. Beads of humidity formed a ring around the seat of my chair.

My plate had three areas of descending darkness. White potatoes cut in polite cubes, tawny parsnips, and livery haggis. It wasn't what I expected. In a tourist shop, I read several recipes for haggis and it was supposed to be stuffed in a sheep stomach. I wanted oats and lungs and liver in a tripe wrap. Kind of the culinary proceeds of a direct mortar hit. One recipe had a picture of a happy tummy giving instructions on how to fill it with offal and oatmeal. I had hoped for a little package I could burst. Oh well, the plate of starch and cholesterol contained heat energy. Maybe enough to start evaporation. I salted it and dug in. The richness and depth of flavor make me feel like I was in bed. For fifteen minutes, I forgot about my wet thighs. I had a pot of tea so I could linger and put off going out. The check came and sat on its little plate like an S.S. officer by the door of the family of deportees. It was inevitable that I had to pay and leave.

My pack had absorbed about ten pounds of water. In addition to the bitterness of leaving the tearoom behind, I had to carry more weight. I trudged out into the diminished tourist flow whose blank looks focused and refocused from shop to shop, and migrated, refugee like, towards the railway station. My destination was London for a couple of days and a quick return. Inside the underheated station, I waited with three Italian girls and their large backpacks for my connection to Edinburgh.

My special fare provided for an overnight trip and the connection was waiting. A boy with an earring and a bandana was seated across from me. He looked like a young punk from Glasgow and was surrounded by bags of fried snacks and two liters of orange soda. We faced each other across the table between the bank of seats and I tried to sleep. After one hour, I was tapped awake by the conductor checking tickets and couldn't get comfortable again. The boy across from me offered a bag of snacks and grinned as the food service ran by and gave us a plastic tray of minimal food and a cold roll. He tossed his roll against the window.

"More crisps? The roll's like a rock, eh?"

"Thanks," I had a chip from a bag labeled "Lamb and Mint Flavored" and tasted it for flavor accuracy. It tasted like musty potato.

"Are you Canadian?"

"No, American."

"I want to go there. It's big. I'm planning a trip for next year. Texas, Arizona, Oregon, then Louisiana."

"In that order?"

"Well, I guess."

"You'll be doing a huge zig-zag. It's about two thousand miles from Louisiana to Oregon. Why don't you start in Louisiana and go to Texas next?"

"I could do that, I really want to go to Texas though. There's somethin' about it."

"Where are you from?"

"Glasgow." It sounded like Galzgoe the way he said it. "I live in Dundee now."

"What's it like?"

"Lots of little people about this high," he gestured with his hand, "Looking for a fight. Go to the wrong area and you get bothered. Short little buggers. I'm a commis chef there, don't get bothered much. I'd like to join the service next."

"What's a commis chef?"

"Sauté, broiler station, you know. Trainee. If I join the armed forces I'll give it up. I'd like to see the world."

"Do you want to leave Scotland?"

"No, but it's wee. Good to go around for a while then settle."

I was totally dry now and could rest warmly. The boy kept talking from his side of the chairs as my attention waned. I coiled up and slept until London.

Chapter Six

Poms

The density and extent of London struck me in comparison to the manageable presence of the Scottish towns and even Edinburgh. It seemed worn out, like a product at the end of its commercial life. The value of it had been extended too far and the market called for a new conception. I stayed in an apartment with a friend for three nights. It must have been three hundred and fifty square feet.

"These flats were part of one home," she explained, "They got split up. Each floor was converted into two flats."

Across the narrow corridor was the door to the neighboring flat. There were two bedrooms and not enough space to open the door to my room if I didn't move the dresser. My friend's family bought it recently.

"How much did you have to pay for this place?"

"About one hundred and forty thousand American."

"Jesus, my father's house is worth less than that at the present exchange rate. His house is a two thousand square foot, brick home with a large yard in an old suburb serving the University where he taught."

"London's expensive. Down payments are low though and long term mortgages are available."

We drove around the neighborhood on the way to where she worked as a research librarian. Lots of Africans were doing errands in bright colored clothing. The intensity of the land use was distressing. I felt anxiety at the density of the population and reduction in the scale of living space.

"What do people think of the black residents around here?"

"There's no real problem. Some people get scared but it's nothing like what I hear goes on in America. We do have those who don't like people who look different, but the main objection is getting to be that there's no more room. This is a *settled* country. Up in Newcastle they're planning new housing. You know Newcastle, coal, armaments, shipbuilding, and steel nearby? Well, all those traditional industries are dead up there, but they still want to build. There are people who go up there to get away from here. And Scotland, we need it for an escape. There's no more country here really. I mean you can go to where you can't see houses and cities and buildings, but the isolation just isn't there any more. Urban feel encroaches on every thing. Look at our cars, little things, if they were any bigger we wouldn't have enough space for housing. The choice is park or live indoors," she laughed.

"You mentioned Scotland. What do they think of increased English visitors?"

"They don't really mind it when we go up. The money helps them. One of their big industries is tourism. You must have seen it when you were up there. In the summer there are crowds of people dressed alike at the Loch Ness Monster Museum. But they don't like it when we stay so well. The English have a history of treating conquered territories and annexations like stepchildren. They use them in their condescending way. Like they're worthy of less consideration than down here. In some ways it's an interesting legal problem. Our Constitution isn't written you know. We have a bunch of documents like the Magna Carta and other historical developments, but nothing with the clarity of your Constitution. What we've created is a little Federal Republic without treating the members as equal partners. There's no passport check when you cross at Berwick, no customs, no nothing. Yet, we treat them like a different country. We tried the poll tax on them first. Like some Nazi experiment, we tried it on the inferior men of the north. Getting back to the Constitutional thing, we don't have clauses and paragraphs that bind us together with equal taxation and commerce rights. The English have drifty notions about Gentleman's agreements and the like but there is nothing that says one area can't be discriminated against economically or that one area, say England, can't isolate itself for the benefit of trade, at the expense of some other region. Say, Scotland. We have precedents, acts, and Parliamentary resolutions, but some things are still unformed."

"England started off with a monarchy which had power wrested from it over ten centuries. Our starting point politically was, 'What can you force the Monarch to concede?' It's different now obviously, but from time to time the highhanded behavior creeps out. I love my leaking little country but it's true. I think there are even three M.P.s who want Scotland to secede. 'Free Scotland,' type thing. No chance. But it's in the mind. It's significant that the idea exists."

"What about the other countries? Wales, Ireland, Northern Ireland?"

"Welsh hate the English more than anyone. The Scots will criticize us and also honestly say they're not anti- English. In Wales they have road signs in Welsh and English and the locals will spray-paint out the English letters. Do you know what it's like to drive when that happens? There was also a spell when English second homes were being burned by resentful locals. The Irish have their independence but Northern Ireland is a violent problem as everyone knows. The Protestants want to stay with England and the Catholics want out. But we treated Ireland like conquered country when we invaded in centuries past. You know, for example, four hundred years ago, Ireland was one, homogeneous country. More or less. Most of the population was Catholic. The Protestants came from the conquerors, like English who colonized Ireland. Anti-Catholic laws were passed to control the majority *and* the Irish Parliament could only make laws of which the English Parliament approved or made themselves. The Protestants held the wealth and power of the country. The legacy remains in Northern Ireland."

"The English Empire is over."

"Yes, yes, but some tendencies and habits remain. A centralized government was very powerful against our neighbors. One of the problems Highland Scotland had was the disunity of its tribes or clans. They had a bunch of separate Kingdoms and political entities in a way. Prince Charles was a unifying figure for them but they had no real tradition of being an organized body. The Chief of the clan expected absolute obedience from his members and the different Clans normally didn't operate together. When they had their uprisings in the seventeen hundreds, even an incompetent like Cumberland could beat them. One of the surprising things about Scotland is that there was a history of gradual Anglicization of the country and peaceable relations from an early age. The early kings of Scotland owned land in England and had to pay homage to English kings. After the Norman invasion of England, the Saxon princess Margaret fled north and married King Malcolm the third. She taught them English customs and institutions. Even more, her sons carried on this tradition. The Celts didn't like it, especially the reorganization of the church along English lines and the suppression of the Celtic monastic orders, but the succession of power centralized authority in the hands of this Anglo-Norman dynasty."

"So why the antagonisms? Why not just a greater England?"

"They were still Scots, of course. They wanted to be separate because they never really trusted these guys to the south. Britons and the like. Mind you, the Scots weren't innocent. They took advantage of the English Civil war to grab English territory in the northeast. But they were proud. Even the vassal Kings couldn't live with their consciences. Robert the Bruce was one. John Balliol was installed by Edward the First as a flunky and couldn't stand it. He turned against his sponsors and made an alliance with England's oldest enemy, France. Ultimately a peaceful union was created early in the nineteenth century. Culloden is sometimes over stated. It was the last gasp of the old Highland tribes. Prince Charles had little support outside of the Highlands. Scotland shot ahead after all the Jacobite business and advanced in commerce, agriculture and intellectual achievements. The history of Scotland since long ago is a gradual weaving with England. Not without rancor and violence. A little romance too."

We parked and my friend went off to work. I walked towards an Underground station, stared at the entangled route map, and memorized my destination. The mechanized gate, which read the magnetic strip on my ticket, seemed out of place in contrast to the potty little English writing on the Underground signs. I went through the gate and down a long escalator to a short corridor, which had a colored staff of destinations for a particular train line. I had to make a choice of going north or south but didn't know where they were. I guessed and went down another flight of stairs to a tunnel that emptied on either side to the train platform. At the end of my Freudian descent I felt buried and disoriented. The smell of machine oil and ozone from the electrical current reminded me of the industrialized trolls called the Eloi in the *Time Machine*. The train compressed a column of air as it arrived and I stepped in among the passengers who silently looked past each other. We rocked quietly to my station and did a tubular escape to an elevator that carried me to daylight. The crowd expanded out of the elevator through the small ticket area and dissipated onto the street. I felt like Jonah out of the whale and looked around to get oriented. Varieties of small shops crowded together like small mammals and leaned against a large department store, which occupied most of a city block. In the early morning light it looked slightly forgotten, despite the foot traffic. Stacks of garbage in plastic bags awaited collection and store owners in their native dress stood outside their businesses, preparing them for the day. In addition to whites there were Pakistanis, Indians and Egyptians. At the end of the street was a building from the eighteen hundreds which housed a public auditorium and Turkish baths. I could feel the nineteenth and twentieth centuries pulling at one another in the contrast of charm and decay. Elegance opposed the need for space and the addition of foreign people. The morning light illuminated the street and the older buildings glowed like an elegant aunt who has become old but is still kind. I walked around a corner past outdoor fruit displays and had coffee in a European style patisserie. As I sat, an eager looking Indian asked if he could use the ashtray at my table. His tie swung lightly as he stood half-bent waiting for my reply.

"Sure."

"Good, thank you. You are not from here, are you?"

"No. U.S.."

"I thought. Neither am I but I live here."

He sat down at the table next to me and turned his chair around so he could see me. "Maybe we are a little alike. What are you doing here?"

"Walking through Scotland."

"Oh my, you are in the wrong place," he laughed, "Did someone give you bad instructions for the underground? A mean trick. You want to be north of here. *North!*"

"I understand, I'm just down here for a few days to work and get some more money for the trip."

"Ah, I see. Who hires you for a couple of days at a time? Hm?"

"Cooking. It's surprisingly available."

"Good, good. What do you think our country, or rather their country in which I live? Ha-Ha."

"It's like an old, used relative. Comfortable, but a little sapped and crowded."

"That is good. True too. You know I am an economist by training. I work in the bureaucracy now. If you think this is crowded, go to Calcutta. You can walk on the bodies."

"What are you doing here?"

"Opportunity, of course."

"What does it look like to an Indian?"

"Well, I am a Brahmin. Do you know what that is? We have power traditionally. To lower Indians, England looks free and organized. But to me, as a Westernized economist, it looks like it's in a little trouble. Let me ask you a question. Who do you think the Indians are most like? Hm?"

"I don't know, there are lots of different ethnic groups."

"Yes, yes, you can tear it apart but come on, answer."

"I don't know, Nepalese?"

"Good guess, at least you didn't choose the Pakistanis. No, the Russians."

"How?"

"We have these feelings of brotherhood. We think sideways and include people. Our worldview is broad. Do you understand?"

"What does this have to do with England?"

"The English also have a group mentality. They like each other, I am not saying they are like Indians because Indian poverty is unimaginably cruel, but they have some similar problems."

"Like what?"

"They are getting crowded on their little island. And as they get economically weaker, they lose their culture a bit. They are getting a bit meaner, more Americanized. For example, people are starting to lie more in business settings. It's not common but it's starting and that English sense of fairness and loyalty to the group is being taxed."

"That's not the only reason."

"Of course not, my good man, but it helps. We are now in a world market you know. Everybody is influenced by everybody else. They lost their empire and their manufacturing base. Do you know Manchester, Leeds?"

"Yes."

"English are quite vulnerable now. Not so independent and being pushed *up* their country like a tube of toothpaste. Ha, ha, do you get it?"

"I do."

"As the invisible hand squeezes the lead tube, they go north to Scotland. *So*, you are doing the right thing. Scotland will be a place of the future for the British."

"What about the European Community, Maastricht?"

"Uncertain, the French are so nasty and I think a common economy is unrealistic. If you were Germany, would you want the rates of your currency to be linked to Portugal, Italy, and Greece? Plus the English are an Island people. De Gaulle didn't want them in the Common Market because he didn't think it would be good for them to get into European problems. He wasn't being mean, he just thought it would create more problems than it would solve. What is your name please?"

"Robert."

"You must let me buy you a pastry, Robert. What a good listener you are. You even have me thinking about the north now. Perhaps I will get a job with private industry and go there to develop a resort. Could you see it? I would learn golf. It's too funny. They eat haggis there don't they?"

"Please ma'm, may I have mango pickle with my haggis? Is that convincing?"

"Can I get you another coffee?"

"Yes please, with chocolate sprinkles." He brought it over.

"I must go, otherwise I will be late. Please don't be insulted."

"No, thanks. What's your name?"

"I am Anant."

"Thanks Anant."

He shook my knee and got up grinning.

"Good luck on your travels. Don't take any wooden dollars. Yes?"

"Nickels."

"Oh, No. Don't take any wooden haggis! Oh, ho!" The door jingled behind him.

I left and walked past a jumble of intimate restaurants. In the space of a half block there was a Spanish place, an Italian trattoria and a French Bistro. They were built up rather than out and had dining areas on two to three smallish floors. As I walked, the commercial district abruptly ended at a traffic circle. I turned left and went along an area of inexpensive hotels made from converted houses. I tried several to determine the range of rates and decided on one with brown shag carpet and mirrored hallways designed to increase the feeling of space in the narrow corridors. I paid a young Indian girl who sat in a small office with three members of her family in a little cluster. As we walked up to my room I noticed that the mirror reflected the carpet and made it seem like the walls were covered in brown rug.

"Who lived here before it was turned into a hotel?"

"I don't know. Someone English." The girl looked at me like I was stupid.

"Lots of Indians own the hotels in this area. They are all similar. Here is the bathroom," she patted a door, "And, here is your room."

Except for the sunlight and high ceilings, it looked like the kind of room a boxer might take during his periods of obscurity. A sink was against the wall and the curtain hung slack on one end of its runner. I could imagine a spinster dying here and as her body was carried out, the carpenters would be moving in to convert the building to separate rooms.

I spent the day going from crowded square to crowded square and had lunch in the smallest dining room in Chinatown. It had ten chairs in two hundred square feet. Another business operated from the front, so the dining area was really one hundred and fifty square feet with four tables. Its kitchen was in the basement. I shared my tiny table with a Chinese woman who showed me how to order. We had wind-dried duck while apologizing to one another for rocking the table on its short leg.

I asked the office to wake me up at seven thirty. The man nodded gravely and gave me my key. In the florescent light my room looked a little more hopeless than it did in natural daylight. The fuzzy yellow blanket looked like it was second hand and the sheets were relaxed from years of laundering (I hoped). In the dark, I listened for strange noises. There were none.

The pounding on my door wakened me from my dream about a catering fiasco. Our van broke down and we had to hire a fleet of taxis to deliver the food. When they arrived the food wouldn't fit in them because of the English design. Over the phone I was explaining to the hostess of the party that I couldn't be expected to know about foreign cars.

"It is Uncle, seven-thirty."

"Thank you."

The breakfast room was in the basement of the hotel and served at a precise hour. I walked past mirrors and a doctor Cagliari staircase to the little cafeteria. A rakish Spaniard with long sideburns and patent leather shoes sat with two female friends who laughed at everything he said. Two Danish girls sat in a corner and quietly spread Danish condiments on their toast. Members of the owners' family were at a large table and ate together like a quiet club. Despite the seediness of the Spaniard and his entourage, I brightened. The temporary presence of people traveling was interesting. I felt the oddness of other places. The sleazy Spaniards were funny. Some tall Germans came in and looked around with disdain. We sat in the same room but no one shared a table with a stranger. Over jiggly poached eggs, we snuck looks at each other.

At the end of three days I spoke with a friend in Newcastle.

"Before you go back up to Scotland, do you want to visit me relatives? I've an uncle in Yorkshire who owns a manor house. We'll meet a friend of mine there and go hill walking."

"Really, a titled person?"

"Not really, used to be the Lord of the Manor meant something, now it's just a name. By the original charter though, he has the right to the virgins of the town. Friday alright?"

I bussed up to Newcastle and we drove past the treeless hills to the worn valleys of North Yorkshire. We went through two gates barring the long gravel road to the house. No one answered our knock and we let ourselves in. An oil stove ran continuously in the kitchen, which was separated from the rest of the house by a long corridor extending through the middle of the house. A living room, dining room, and other spaces hung like separate appendages along the spine of the corridor. It was a house in a line.

"Strange design, how did this happen?"

"Each room is separately heated," said Ben, "If they aren't being used, they don't want the expense of fuel. Kitchen always stays warm because it's the heart of the house."

Instructions were left for dinner on a note. A warm lamb casserole was waiting and there were vegetables to heat. As we arranged the food, a solid, fresh-faced young man came down stretching and yawning. We were introduced then he opened his mouth with a smile and began talking on several topics for the next ten minutes.

"What do you think, Bob?"

I hadn't been listening to the whole thing, but he wanted an answer. His manner was imperious and a little adversarial. I pulled out a reply, which provided the subject matter for his next five-minute monologue at the end of which he looked over his properly held utensils and flexed his nostrils with conceit.

"What do you think of what I've just said," his face asked, "Pretty good, yes?"

His sense of rightness and confidence would have been unbearable if it wasn't offset by the compulsiveness of his conversation, which betrayed a little vulnerability. I wondered how my friend Ben managed with the guy. He was quiet and elicited confidence by his absence of unnecessary speech. The friend carried on as if he was in a public forum. We went to the living room where he asked me questions about the U.S., then commented on my answers. It was comical the way he appropriated and directed conversation. He finished his statements with a sneer of pleasure and fulfillment from the experience of his own speech. I couldn't help liking him. He was imperial and sociable at the same time. I disappeared upstairs and fell asleep in my clothes.

At breakfast the next morning Ben's friend carried on as if he were the owner. During breaks in the din, I was undistracted from the ambience of English country living. We tapped poached eggs and listened to the stove groan as it expanded and contracted. The house was a solid stone safe area with paintings of ancestors and photos of recent generations in their public school ties.

"What did your family do, Ben? It looks like your relatives had wealth."

"Carpets. In Halifax. It's strange to go there. Parks are named after us. You see statues with your name on them."

"What happened?"

"Business went bad."

"What does your uncle do now?"

"He never was in the business. He was always a farmer. Now he gets paid a lot to not grow things. We've too much food. The government will subsidize non-production. He also rents pasture to sheep owners and has developed and sold some summer homes on the land. Clever fellow. No university, but you wouldn't know it from talking to him."

We drove along a one-lane road with turnouts for oncoming traffic. The hills got steeper and limestone started to show through. At a parking lot we put on our boots with the other hill walkers. It looked like an athletic team with members of various ages dressing to go up the paths. In the hills we passed people going up and down. It was not a private nature experience.

"What do you think of our Dales, Bob?" asked Ben's friend.

"Worn out, old. Lots of people."

"Ungrateful foreigner! Name three things Americans have done this century of lasting importance."

"Saved you and the rest of Western Europe in World War II."

"Besides that, that's not a thing. Inventions, I meant."

"I'm not doing this."

"Ha, there, see, you couldn't. Could you? What are you in England for any way?"

"An interest in Scotland."

"Like what."

"General."

"How have you found them?"

"A little less standoffish than the English."

"What else?"

"They complain about the English a little. Like the poll tax for instance. They claim it was tried out on them a full year ahead of the English."

"What a blather of nonsense. They complain like we're imperialists, which we are, or were, but the poll tax was a replacement for the rates. Property taxes. Property was going to be reassessed and rates were going to rise. A lot of old people on fixed incomes were going to be taxed too much on their properties. Their income couldn't adjust to the higher rates. Did they want to be taxed out of their property? Of course not. The government in London thought it might be better to try a head tax instead. Lots of the Scottish M.P.s rushed down to get an alternative to the rates. It wasn't discrimination." Six people filed by on the muddy track.

"What do you think of that, Bob?"

"Hm."

"Come on now, back to your country. Name three things."

"Tasty food, green vegetables and used prophylactics."

"Funny, funny man. I knew you couldn't answer. That's the way you North Americans are. When I was in the Himalayas I noticed that a girl standing in front of me at the hostel registration signed her name then listed her nationality as 'French, from Canada.' What a load of rubbish. I picked up the book and told her, 'You're not French from Canada, you're fucking Canadian of French descent. Why are you writing this stuff?' She went out of her mind and started screaming at me in that French Canadian way."

He bared his front teeth and made a chopping gesture with his molars to imitate the girl's accent.

'I don't think it's your business to say what I am. We are French and are different from the English in Canada and blah, blah and on and on. She was out of her mind.' It was easy to imagine him grabbing the book and appropriating her identity in an attempt to enforce his own interpretation of things. His imitation of her accent was hilarious. He didn't bother to wait for a response.

"Watch this! I'm going to go down the hill using a technique I learned from a Sherpa in Nepal. Watch!" He went down the hill in large steps.

"Good, eh?" he called up.

At dinner we sat in the main dining room with a fourth guest who was a friend of the family. I snuck looks at her beautiful profile as I sat next to her. Ben's friend was excellent at maintaining interest in the continuous story of Ben's aunt, about her enrollment in University as a mature student. His uncle was telling the other half of the table about the European Community and currency rates. He looked over and changed the subject.

"Ben tells me you're interested in Scotland."

"Yes."

"To understand them, you have to know they are Presbyterians."

"Someone told me it doesn't matter."

"They are wrong. The different religions haven't polarized into warring groups, but the character of the people is influenced by Presbyterianism. Look at their buildings. You can feel it. Sensible, direct, unadorned, but not without good will," he stared at his plate for a moment. "Do you understand Presbyterian doctrine?"

"Sure, Calvinistic. Predestination with limited redemption. The ideas conflict."

"Yes, but the religious culture is there. You can sense it. The Scots are not sensualists. Their food is even plainer than ours."

"It's not just from poverty?"

"One of the doctrines of Presbyterianism is the total depravity of man and the necessity to control it."

"I'm listening."

"They don't like strong centralized control. The highest authority they have is the elder."

"How is that in contrast with somewhere else?"

"The Episcopalians go back to ancient Bishops. The Bishop ministers to a large population under them. Presbyterians have much more localized organization. It's independent. They're so independent, they keep subdividing into miniscule parts. If they didn't stop they would have become a million individuals scowling in opposite directions with their arms folded. Have you heard of the 'Wee frees'? You find them on the Hebrides. They give you a dirty look if you drive your car on Sunday. The ferry companies have to make their schedules around their preferences regarding the Sabbath."

"You feel this was that significant?"

"I don't know, maybe the religion just suits their nature. Maybe they chose it because of what they are. It's there."

"Here the buildings look functional and faceless. Old leaden stone. How is it different in Yorkshire?"

My neighbor leaned on the table and answered, "We're Church of England around here," she said. "It's a church that accommodates a wide range of religious commitment. It doesn't really have an identity any more, it kept softening doctrine to keep up with social and economic changes through the decades. It's as if the morality of Christ can be changed if the social cost of it gets too high."

Uncle returned.

"Presbyterianism is not like that. Its history is more skeptical of social influences. It resists. Stubborn. Bad tempered in its original conception. Shrinks and subdivides to *maintain* doctrine."

"The Scots I met were helpful."

"John Calvin was not a pleasant guy. Not many laughs. He didn't mind beheading what he considered a heretic. Or burning them. He also liked power."

"Scots don't seem overwhelmed by their church."

"That was one of their big fights. Calvin had enormous power over his church. He tried to administer all local matters and control the social and individual life of the people. Later on, the Scots had a big argument about the amount of power, which could be centralized in their religion. They limited it. They also made sure that no political body could appoint its clergy. They left the State and its practice of patronage. Around eighteen-forty I think."

"Sounds like a way of avoiding English infiltration."

"Always an issue for those fellows. Can I get you anything?"

He set out a glass of port and two small cordial glasses of cherry brandy and Crème de Menthe. I sipped the port and tried the cherry brandy. The Crème de Menthe glowed like an angry green emetic. I would hurl a sticky wash over the table if I even smelled it, so I left it as far from my place as possible. Fresh mince tarts and hard sauce were brought in. I felt my pancreas brace itself for the sugar assault. In an attempt to acknowledge their generosity and hide my pathetic inability to drink, I picked at a tart and drank black coffee.

"Oh! Look at Bob's drinks. We could make a traffic light. It's an actual drink you know!" Ben's friend extended his presence to our side of the table. Uncle smiled.

"You use Crème de Menthe, Irish Cream and cherry brandy at the top. Need a bartender with a steady hand. They're fun!"

He bestowed his smile on all of us. I reeled at the thought. I hoped my body's supply of insulin would hold out through the evening. The heat was shut off and we moved to the living room. The change in temperature refreshed me a little. I glanced with chagrin at the liquor display on the corner table.

"Would you like a little Scotch, Bob?" Aunt offered.

I thought of another poison permeating my body. It looked old, though.

"It's an old single malt. Since I stopped smoking I like a drink. Yes?"

Aunt waited. I was caught between wanting to experience the quality of the stuff and the potential damage to the handsome wool carpet if it didn't agree with me. It looked expensive. This was a good offer.

"Yes," fell out of my head. My organs flexed for one more secretion. The conversation turned back to the European community and Ben's friend flogged the same question at Uncle after receiving a satisfactory explanation. Uncle was patient. Civilization was wearing at me. I went to the kitchen to get an apple, which I hoped would act as a mitigating body in my stomach. In bed I dreamed of a pizza I couldn't swallow.

Chapter Seven

Mr. Plod

A sere glaze of sunlight colored the green hills in Pitlochry on my return. It was a different town today, softened by the weather and brightly lit through the clear air. I finished my coffee and discussed the custom of tipping with the owner as he closed his shop at five P.M.

"People don't think we have it, but we do! Ten per cent is fine," he said hopefully. We looked at my map and he made suggestions about where to camp.

"Ignore the trespassing laws. Camp where I tell you. You'll have no problems."

As I closed my map he gave me his card and a package of two scones and butter.

"They're free. Send me a card from the west when you get there. Good walking."

I went up a hill for a mile, then went due west towards the narrow fiord-like Lochs of Tummel and Rannoch. The country was steeper and more forested than the grasslands to the east. I passed the clearing of a caravan park, then entered the shadow of the forest. Flecks of blue and gold were visible through the trees and the condensation on the grass dampened my boots. I crossed peat colored streams and went up and down compact hills for eight miles. It was nine O'clock and there was plenty of light. The day was so comfortable and the light so benevolent that it was like walking indoors.

I started to look for a place to camp. Loch Tummel was silent. There were no boats or bathers on the lake or the shore. A small opening in the bushes was the start of a path that led to a grassy ledge three feet above a pebble beach. I looked around for signs which said "No overnight camping" or any other indications that someone might come along and enforce trespassing laws. There were none, so I pushed through the narrow opening and set down my pack.

I began my routine, which consisted of setting up my tent and getting everything spread out. I checked to make sure my bedding was right, then sat there. In the end I always sat there, wherever I was, in silence. It was anticlimactic. I wanted a fire, hot food, a companion. I kicked some dead wood to break it into pieces and my foot bounced off the grey limb. I hacked at it with my five-inch knife and lost patience. When I foraged I found nothing dry or small enough to use. In consolation I had a sesame cracker with a tomato. The juice made my hands cold. There was no more warmth in the light. It was a little too dark to read and when I tried it hurt as my pupils continuously adjusted. I lay down in the tent to sleep but it was boring. Plain and green inside. I wasn't sleepy. I got out and stared at the silent lake. The silence and absence of development on the shores made it primitive, but the light forests which covered the tall narrow hills through which it ran made it unthreatening and domestic. The other side of the lake was close. I could see details on the other shore. Nothing seemed unknowable or lurking about this area. My little spot was almost landscaped. The tent was pitched on short green grass considerately located off the stones of the beach. The complete absence of animal life was eerie. The idyll seemed artificial. Unexpectedly a fish jumped and I felt better. Company. "Hi! I see you! Would you like a tomato?"

Appreciation quickly turned to opportunism and I decided to try to catch it. I ran to my pack for the hand line, which was weighted and ready to use. I unrolled a length of line and threw the hook and sinker toward the spot where I saw the fish. The sinker went ahead of the hook, which caught my sweater and wound my arm and shoulder in nylon while the weight dangled by my elbow. So much for poaching. In the waning light I tried to get the barbed hook through the fabric of my sweater. It was eleven O'clock. I reached down with my hand to grab the material around my forearm where the hook was. It was uncomfortable and as I worked the hook in this spastic contortion, I started to get a headache from concentrating my vision. I sat down to have a minor tantrum and ground my molars as I yanked the hook. Four long strands of yarn left the body of my sweater and drooped. The hook came out covered with black fuzz. My bottom became cold as I sat there so I retreated to the tent where I lay down and waited for my embarrassment to subside in the dark green oblivion. The cold leached through my ground cloth and chilled the center of my back as I lay awake and listened to the fish make happy wet sounds as it jumped.

The morning was bright. The clarity of the air didn't diffuse the natural light and everything looked like it was on display. There was almost no moisture under the tent so I packed and moved out quickly. For a mile I went through the park like setting and stopped at a hotel in the shape of a small castle. I crushed my way through the expanse of gravel driveway and shook off my pack. Inside it was silent. A small table held some brochures advertising the Tummel Forest. The front room was as large as a small bungalow and paneled in oak. In an adjoining room was a small fire and some cookies left next to an empty coffee holder. I picked them up and wrapped them in a napkin for future consumption. The bar was dark and club like. In the large dining room one couple ate breakfast. I knocked on the kitchen door. A small grey man appeared.

"Can I help you?"

"Is breakfast available for non-guests?"

"No, sorry."

"You're not busy, can I get anything?"

"Coffee and biscuits in the sitting room."

I went back to where I was originally and waited for my own cookies and coffee. Rain appeared and spattered the windows. There were three cars in the drive and two diners at eight thirty in the morning. The stillness of the place made me restless and I wanted more to eat. The small service came and I had it in silence while reading a brilliant collection of articles which showcased Spanish thinkers. I searched for the owner and paid him. When I felt it was safe I pushed the magazine up my loose sweater and walked towards the door. The owner was standing in the entrance as if he was waiting for me and watched as I left. What was the problem? I had only stolen twice in forty-five minutes.

I put on my vaguely wet pack and almost immediately walked by the Loch Tummel Visitor's center and Queen's View Museum. Tourists milled around the small buildings while a "real" craftswoman practiced her skill on a wood sculpture. In the small museum were displays about the reforesting project for the area and an explanation about the origin of the name for this location. Queen Victoria once visited here and according to one plaque, even had to endure the hardship of one or two cold meals. People pulled in and out of the center in gentle car queues. I bought some post cards and walked on.

At dusk I reached Kinloch Rannoch. Since dark was around ten o'clock, everything was closed in the small town. I had a beer in the local hotel and asked about the price of a room. Forty pounds for a single. It was dark as I went back to the road and read the plaque on a statue commemorating some Highland historical event as I decided what to do. On the map was a commercial campground three miles to the east. I didn't want to walk any more. I had come twenty-three kilometers, and my feet hurt. A street lamp illuminated the small square where I stood. It was silent and deserted. I continued west for five hundred yards, then decided to go back in the direction from where I came. For a while I stood there with my thumb out to get a ride. Nothing happened. A group of adolescents came by and stared at my efforts which must have seemed senseless. I may as well have been hitching in the Gobi desert. After a while, a V.W.

van went by the square where I had been and turned down the road towards the camping area. It was better to be at the square so I put on my pack and walked there. No more cars came by. I walked back west to where I had been standing and kept going before I was arrested for vagrancy. Or lack of intelligence.

After a mile I reached the eastern shore of Loch Rannoch and walked along the dense foliage near the bank. It was dark among the trees and I could no longer see beyond twenty feet. The banks were steep and there was nowhere to camp. After two miles I saw a clearing with short heather and felt the ground for tent adequacy. Did I become stupid as daylight waned? Would I have to plan ahead for each night to avoid diminished judgment at twilight? It wasn't as if I were going too fast. The tent hung from its posts like laundry. I got in and pushed the floppy fabric from around my body. A sesame cracker was not sufficient solace for my fatigue. Maybe I needed a Sherpa to keep this from happening; someone to gently nudge me when circulation to my brain seemed to be reduced. I rolled over on my glasses and felt their twisted shape. Sleep was too good for me at this point. I deserved penance, but I was too tired to get out and do a wilderness *Auto-de-fe*. Self-punishment could be arranged tomorrow. I would turn myself in to a local Eugenics society who would cull me from the race to prevent this from happening to future generations.

In the morning I got up and looked at my camp. It looked like a pile of unwashed clothes. The tent sagged listlessly and my gear was thrown around in a demoralized clutter. A sign directly above my pile read, "No Overnight Stays." Sue me. Go ahead. Collect me and put me in a Scottish jail. They'd like me. It would be interesting for them to talk to a foreigner. I bet a small village incarceration would be pleasant. Someone from out of town would excite the residents. I could tell them stories of strange places I have seen, like Newark, New Jersey or Gary, Indiana. Special food would be provided for me until my sentence was done, then perhaps a small job would be created so I could stay around because I had become so popular. The stays from my tent interrupted my reverie, and snapped against the nylon. They were loose and as I pulled up the stakes the tent collapsed. I looked at it and sympathized. I didn't want to be responsible anymore either. When everything was packed up I leaned my pack tidily against a tree. It looked more alert than I did. "Now what?" it asked. A treat, I decided.

A mile back, I had passed a small development in the dark. In the light I saw several buildings I hadn't seen last night. It was a time-share development and looked like something on the Northern California coast, set back on the steep hills. Time-shares seemed all wrong. This was still little Scotland. Time-share sounded like a place for profligate oil sheiks or Americans with aviator sun glasses and bovine girlfriends to come and have glossy sex and consumption junkets. The coming and going would ruin the brittle domesticity of the area.

A long asphalt track led to the restaurant-hotel. I walked in and watched for smart professionals wearing pagers and portable cellular phones. There were none. The construction was new but the lobby had the erect no-nonsense feel of Scottish architecture. The buildings and the people dining had the feeling of warmth and economy of style. A happy hostess with pleasantly jumbled teeth came forward and seated me. She wore a long dark skirt, maroon sweater and a tie. Sensible looking black, low heel shoes completed her matronly outfit which surprisingly enhanced and gave focus to her freckled, cheerful face.

I went over and stared at the buffet. The selection of pale, fresh fruits looked like they had never seen the sun. I took some stewed prunes and two miniature bags of meusli back to my table, which was by a bay window, and set with two small jars of marmalade, a tall plaid can of oatcakes, butter squares, cream and sugar and a toast rack. I was surrounded by comfort items and life came back to me. I wondered for a moment if food was better company than humans. The girl came back with my personal carafe of coffee and stood by me smiling. I thought of asking her if she would mind if I put my head in her stomach and left it there for a minute. It would be a perfect addition to the warmth of the food.

Smoked fish came with eggs and pink ham on an oven hot plate. I sat there, on the tartan rug with the spindly ash furniture, until they took down the breakfast buffet.

––––––––––

Loch Rannoch didn't have the intimacy of Loch Tummel. It rained a sloppy spatter as I went along its shores. A woman served me late afternoon coffee and explained how Scottish property law worked.

"It's feudal."

"How?"

"You don't own the land, you own the building. The Laird owns the land. A tenant pays rent for puttin' his property on the land."

"Why would any one want to build under these conditions?"

"It's changed. The law allowed people to buy the land from the Laird for seven years' taxes. Our tax rate was so low we bought our plot of land for forty-seven pence. But that was after paying a lot of years' ground rents. Things are more equal now. Our law is different than English law. It's behind as far as property is concerned."

"Can you feel much English influence here?"

"It's getting so you can't find a hotel not owned by the English," she charged forward a little, "They think we come out of the Heather with our kilts, but we know they don't treat us as equals. There's the poll tax, bad roads and when there's a war, they always send in the Scots first against the enemy."

I wasn't about to argue and turned to look at the rain.

Two hours down the road I stopped at a guesthouse managed by a German who didn't speak English. The door was locked and a sign said to ring the bell for access. When the hostess answered she motioned for me to come in and I followed her through the ghostly white house to a narrow, barely adequate area used for dining. I was the only guest and it was silent. Access to the other rooms was controlled and all the doors were shut. It was as if they were trying to save everything for some other occasion, some future moment that took place after life. I ordered a mineral water and plum cake. The effervescence was loud in the stillness of the closet-like room and when the sun came out it lit everything like a cemetery on a clear spring day. Inside, the clean white and pastel blue walls gleamed with indifference to life. I picked at my cake and imagined an embalmed body in the next room. The door to this little dining area was shut. Life was subordinate to the maintenance of order here. It wasn't the direct, economical hominess of Scottish hospitality. Air would have been nice too. As an act of defiance, I didn't finish my cake. They couldn't cram me in some compartment. What could they do? Tell me I couldn't have dessert? The drama inside my head was interrupted when the hostess opened the door and asked me if I wanted a meal. I declined and paid her for my order, then went through the locked front door to the long exit path.

At the Ericht stream, the landscape broadened and cleared. The west end of Loch Rannoch was more exposed than the eastern section. Wide quiet beaches of pebble and sand made the area a little more desolate. A small stone tower had been built offshore. Its miniature scale and the immersion of its foundation in the Loch made it look like a mistake. As if the builders had missed the intended site on the first attempt and built there because no one had told them to stop. A small, quiet grocery sat on the end of the Loch, tended by a man from Yorkshire. It had three small tables for light refreshments and a rack with pamphlets about the clans who were active in this area. The tower at one time had been used to imprison a member of the MacGregor clan, who were definitely the bad boys of the area. They were slightly nomadic, without the patience for agricultural life, and tended towards raiding and hunting. In the area there was also a rock used as the worktable for a clan chief who consecutively crushed the heads of his woman's children over a disappointment in their relationship. On the map, Prince Charlie's cave was marked eight miles due north. A mother and her adolescent son sat at the table next to me having dessert. The bell attached to the door rang from time to time as customers entered to shop and chat with the owner. It would be silent, then the bell would ring and people would tap around the hard floor before it became silent again. When I asked about a place to sleep the owner went outside. "There's a man in a tractor out there. Talk with him about a place to sleep."

I went out and looked up at a round guy with gaps in his teeth. He looked me over and told me he owned a caravan park.

"I'm camping," I explained.

"Can't do it then, I'd get in trouble with my contract. Caravans only," he ruminated for a second. "But go ahead and sleep on my land. Keep it clean mind you!"

He gave me directions to a rocky field next to the river Gaur. I chose a place out of the way of sheep droppings and set up close to the banks. I gathered firewood and went back to the entrance of the pasture. From the gate, I could see the rocky, green fields bump down east to the Loch and behind them were the high glaciated hills forming the narrow Loch valleys. I hadn't looked behind me before and all of this looked new, even though I had spent three days walking through it. The evening light was clear and had an odd lavender-gold hue. The long steep hills were jumbled together along the scooped depression of the Lochs like boys of various sizes clustering around a clearing. They jostled and climbed one another for access to the center. The Druidic green fields touched the tan grass at the base of the close hills which were swept up to their summits in lavender heather. Patches of green forest covered some of the land, and the grey clouds offset the heather so that each gained depth of color. The whole thing was washed in copper and blue light from the sky. Sub-Alpine was giving way to sub-Arctic at this spot and the hills and sky beat against each other in a soft vibration. The flames from the fire were insignificant in this airless, amber clarity which exposed everything. I took out my pint of Scotch and skewered some green olives over the fire. For dinner I had hot olives and Scotch as I stared east.

Chapter Eight

Rannoch Primitif

I packed up in the cloudy, plain morning and went towards the town of Rannoch Station where roads and paths stopped. I wanted to catch a train south and then continue walking west. The way was slightly undulating and unpopulated. A primitive lake sat unused in the indifferent tundra surroundings. The sky darkened and made the area seem even more isolated. Rannoch had a hotel, a couple of houses and a rail station over a bridge. I didn't want to go on so I sat in the tearoom by the tracks and let a train go by. I ordered a scone and tea and got interested in the labels of snacks which were on display. I was tired and didn't feel like making plans for the next part of the trip. When I ready I would go.

Leisurely, I studied a raisin in my scone and rolled it around. For variety's sake, I walked to the hotel and asked for lunch. A man with a black moustache said it wasn't available until twelve O'clock and it was only eleven fifty. He looked me directly in the eye and said I'd have to wait ten minutes. A display of fishing hooks was against the wall and I asked to buy some. He curtly told me I needed a permit to fish and which house in town was the office where they were sold. I went to the washroom and hoped he wouldn't burst in to tell me that it was for dining customers only. I returned to the tea room by the train station, then recrossed the bridge and dawdled in the red outdoor phone booth from where I called someone I knew wasn't home so I could see what the Scottish operators sounded like. A gate leading to a loch had a sign by it so I went over and read it. It said, "Public Road to Glencoe."

No! What unwelcome information. The day was going to be spent taking a lazy train ride and them sleeping inside. At the tearoom, I opened my map. The road was not on it. Deceiver. A round fellow in a sweatshirt told me it was fourteen miles and could be boggy. The fruit slices looked good so I bought one and pouted over it. It was not sufficient solace though and as I slipped on my pack I decided to get two more as special recognition for meeting my walking obligations. As I passed the gate, the sun came out and lit the grey and green landscape in white light. A broad track took me to a crest overlooking Loch Laidon. A small sunny beach, with fine white sand, was to my right. The scale of it fit the Scottish summer. A tiny little place for a tiny little period of warmth. In the grass nearby, a plaque had been erected; I went over and bent down to read it.

> Neil, forgive me if you are leaving.
> For you beloved my life, if you have died
> All the leaves will fall on my breast
> It will rain on my soul all night and all day
> My feet will want to move where you are sleeping
> But I shall go on living.
>
> Jayne
> 14-4-92

A public display of private emotion. I looked over at the high brooding hills to the west. Their tall oval shapes shrouded in the wet air gave them the appearance of somber, perpetual barriers to their region. Where I stood the sun weakly brightened the shores in thin white light. The expression of the plaque seemed as fragile as the light in this exposed lake plain. It was in good shape and no one had written "fuck" on it or defaced it. I wondered why she put it here. Stray walkers didn't know her and she probably had friends or family to confide in. Perhaps the scope of the exchange she had with individuals wasn't sufficient. She had to appeal to the identity of this area which was at her core. People just weren't enough.

The sun went in and came out. I followed the dirt path to the shores of the loch where it dead ended without further instructions. I turned and walked back in the direction I already came a half-mile. A locked cattle gate with a little stair on its side led to the only other path I could find. I went up the three wooden stairs, straddled the fence, and went down three rungs to a broad dry path that went up and down among a local evergreen forest. After a steep descent, the path ended abruptly and deposited me among grassy clusters of black earth and water. A narrow way led through the wet, but it was constantly necessary to improvise and plan dry routes around submerged areas. I hopped thick brooks, stopped and started over miniature peat islands, and made an irregular ascent to a ridge aimed directly at Glen Coe. Even at the top of the hills, the ground was soaked. Water came from the earth like a liquid will that claimed the ground. No buildings were in sight any longer.

The middle of Loch Laidon was three quarters of a mile to my left, past undulating patches of low heather and grass. Directly across from me was a cove with sandy patches surrounded by short cliffs. I worked my way down to the bank to some rocks and threw in my hand line and bait. Nothing. The sky turned charcoal as I waited for a fish. I wound up my line and cast again. Nothing. To leave, I walked over a high knoll to a miniature delta covered in black silt. My footsteps through it revealed white sand under the blackness. The wet silt sucked at my boots and I hopped onto a pile of small boulders set in the sand. The shore was a primitive miniature of local geology. Like one of those water-filled scenes you shake and watch the snow swirl around the inside. My feet twisted as I jumped off and landed on the uneven ground, then followed the flank of a purple hill towards the track. The ascending hills changed shape quickly and every fifty to one hundred yards I had to change direction. I followed ridges, coasted over gentle purple swellings and sweated up the uneven sides of the worn valley. I wanted to run but the ground wasn't regular. At the top, water continued to flow. It started to rain so I put on a poncho and dodged rivulets and staggered through large swampy areas.

At dusk I reached an old dirt drover's road which confidently led around small hills and over loud streams. After one and a half hours the road entered the wide valley floor of Glen Coe and wound through it like a string laid across a rug. The fence of a private residence abruptly ended passage on the road. With impatience I followed a soaked track around the perimeter of the property, fell down a steep stream bed and came to the unfenced, paved continuation of the road. Night was falling and the dim light in the distance became an increasingly important, comfort promising beacon. A car came towards me and stopped. The driver rolled down his window and asked me not to camp until I passed the final gate out of his property. Rain popped on the rubberized top of my waterproof as I listened. The electric window rolled up and I stood there blankly for a second. It was pouring. I didn't want to camp in this weather. He may as well have told me not to eat the grass. A mile further I opened the metal gate and squished the last half mile to the hiker's lounge of the only hotel in the area. I felt scolded by the weather, like I had been switched by a stern schoolmistress to remind me that I wasn't so great.

"You're not in charge," said the rain as it leached heat from me. The hiker's accommodation was in the "unpreferred" part of the building, behind the public bar for non-hikers. In the vestibule I shook off my poncho and hung it up. My body immediately lost ten degrees and I sprang through the second door into the lounge. It was relieving. The adequate heat surprised me and I liked the feeling that this jumble of soggy hikers in their stocking feet and dirty gear was my group. Old mountaineering equipment was on display in small cases and there were pictures of expeditions setting out thirty and forty years ago. I ordered a hot soup and felt for the effects of each spoonful as they dropped satisfaction, a spoon at a time, into my body. It was like sex in a bowl and I was absorbed in it. Some Germans sat at my table and interrupted my focus. I looked up with a demented look which must have made them uncomfortable. They moved back a little on their bench and delicately asked how to order the soup. The couple looked so fragile and tidy. I decided to help them, even though it meant putting down my spoon. The soup came and their curly hair bobbed up and down against their crinkly, nylon windbreakers as they gratefully ate.

I had counted on a room for the night and asked how much they were. The waiter told me forty pounds a night, which I couldn't afford, and I sat stunned in at the prospect of putting on my wet boots and setting up my tent in the cold rain. This disappointment left me temporarily catatonic and I sat as long as I could until the bell rang for closing. Outside I cursed and sputtered as I handled the cold metal supports to the tent.

The sun heated the ground moisture into a light vapor which steamed me awake. I sat up in the hot haze and looked at a pile of brown sugar in the corner. How did *that* get there? I didn't have any. I got closer and saw that it was a dense cluster of flying insects, smaller than the holes in my mosquito netting. As I bent down I was bitten thirty five times on my face. The swarm came to life and filled up my tent like a gas. They found every exposed part of my body, and as I swatted them they bit the backs of my hands. Within thirty seconds I was out of control and fell out of the tent clutching what I could like a refugee fleeing a war. Outside was no better. Over the bright green grass the barely distinguishable midges flew like substitute air in an inescapable medium of torment. My sleeping bag, poncho and tent were draped over my head and arms as I trudged around trying to find a place away from them. I drifted around for a while look-ing like a derelict dressed in old bedclothes. My down coat was still on but I wasn't going to take anything off. I put the poncho over my head and felt the heat soar under enough clothes for Arctic conditions. Everybody was afflicted. The grounds looked like an asylum as people dressed in camping equipment and towels went around flailing the air and running and stop-ping for no apparent reason.

Peering through the slit I folded in the poncho, I rolled up my gear which took four times as long as usual, and struck at the pests. When it was done I rested my pack against a stone bridge and ran into the hotel restaurant. I stayed there for two hours while I pleasantly watched their life cycles end and tapped goodbye to them through the window by my table.

The loaf-like hills of The Glen were sunny today and a rich brown as I stood, welt covered, hitch hiking due south to Dalmally. There was nothing tragic about the area now. It just felt old. The tall humps must have been Alp-like before they were eroded by ice and water. A large tractor-trailer carrying logs came to an abrupt stop a little way down the road. I could smell brake asbestos as I stood next to the tire and spoke to the driver. I climbed in and we bounced along as he cheerfully explained the timber industry and told me of the time he spent planting trees on these hills with his father and his brother.

"You can do two thousand in a day," he said.

It sounded like a lot of work. At Dalmally I didn't notice the height of the cab and fell to the ground after jumping from six feet. I lay sprawled on the asphalt while the driver looked over and smiled.

"Are you alright?" he asked.

I blushed and looked sheepish as the driver handed me my pack while pointing to the inn he recommended. We were stopped right in front of it. I walked up the steep drive and past the pub part of the hotel to the main entrance. Inside was quiet like a private residence and the air crackled softly in the emptiness. I rang a bell by the small table that served as a reception area and a woman on the far side of middle age entered. Soft good will pressed from her substantial cheeks and I followed her into the parlor for a sandwich and tea. When it came, the sandwich was surprisingly like the woman; soft centered and comfortable. Her slightly aquiline nose dipped gently as we spoke. She asked about the U.S. and gave her opinions on religion. I asked her about the clans in this area.

"Clans don't matter like they used to. I'm a MacGregor on my mother's side, but no one really cares. A greater problem is that I'm half English and raised there. The locals here are very insulated and don't go anywhere.

They get threatened by outsiders and often stand in our pub and make loud insults. Towards us and our guests."

Her husband came in and sat on the sofa in a comfortable black sweater and pants.

"Young people in general today don't know how to behave. They go to a dance dressed in their Wellies, right from the barnyard. Standing there with their mud."

His wife added, "It was better before, young people had respect for manners and proper dress. I think the young do it now just to shock. That's the idea, isn't it?"

Their conversation was a little disappointing. I asked about clans again.

"The whole area used to be forested. It was all cut down for sheep raising. The MacGregors had a bad reputation but eventually they settled. Lots of MacLeods around too, especially toward the Islands of Mull and Iona," said husband.

"We don't think of those things so much any more up here. Now it's history, isn't it?" I felt I had to respond each time she said "Isn't it" but it was just rhetorical. I stopped nodding and she continued in her deliberate, velvet will, "More important is work for our young. Very often they've nothing to do, or aren't willing to do it. We have social services that actually give money to people who want to start businesses. People complain about lack of work but it's there for people who really want it. Nowadays it's a matter of trying, isn't it, and people don't do what they need to do to work. They become a burden on the allotment."

Her nose dipped gently as she smiled and finished her sentence. She brought me another pillow-like sandwich and sat in the light by the window, watching my zealous consumption with contentment. I wasn't getting much information about the clans; she and her husband reminisced about times past and told me about the increased tourism in the area.

"Too many golf courses. A fellow put one in here and not enough people came. There's too many and posher ones than his," said husband.

It became dark and I went over to the lounge part of the inn and sat at a barstool. The small, dark barmaid told me she was from Liverpool when I asked her about her accent.

"Why did you come here?"

"No jobs in Merseyside. I liked it though, I miss it."

She really did. Her momentary, faraway look made me feel that she longed for her home. I told her I needed a bed for the night and she quickly took up the phone and called some places for me.

"Call this number later, she's not home now, but try in an hour."

"How did you end up here, in this little town?"

"I was traveling through and needed a job. A friend got me this one. It's good here, the country and all, but I'm a Scouser."

"What's that?"

"Liverpool native, we're kind of a group."

"Different from Londoners?"

"Oh, yes, we'll talk to each other," she laughed.

I moved towards a table four people were leaving. I wanted to eat on a chair with a back. Just as I got off my stool a sturdy blonde man and his girlfriend sat where I wanted to go. I took the table behind it instead and hit the ice cubes in my drink with a swizzle stick. A big wooly fellow came over towards the table I originally wanted.

"I'm Cubby McCann, and I'm the best of four!" he exclaimed and stood directly behind the square blonde head of the seated man.

"Have I taken your place?" the seated man asked politely.

"Mm. You have." Cubby wobbled a bit and looked at him with watery eyes.

"Sorry, it looked like your party left. Should we move?"

His girlfriend looked over at Cubby with her perpetually surprised look.

"I'm the best of four. Some say they're the very best of all, but I'm the best of four. It's enough! Sit down! Look, look at this. I'm the man who did this."

He pulled out an article and waved it around then dropped it at the blonde man's place who courteously read it and raised his eyebrows.

"You're a good man, you saved a sea otter."

"Aye, I'm the trawler captain who pulled the otter out of the net. Do you want to arm wrestle?"

His hands were as big as hub caps.

"No, I'm with my lass now thanks." He was a gentleman who looked like he could give the man a challenge but preferred to save his power.

"Sorry," he bellowed, "Didn't mean to bother the lass." Cubby looked over at me and pursed his lips. I guess he decided I was too small a morsel with which to trouble.

"I'll be going now. Ha! I'm the best of four."

Chapter Nine

Religion is nice

The only route to my next destination, Oban, was along a busy highway. Cars and trucks blew by me as I stepped up and down the high shoulder of the road to avoid traffic. Steep hills descended into Oban and the ferry dock, which had a modern, mall-like tourist center. Mannikins in tartans and sweaters stared out into nowhere from plate glass windows. Inside a dozen glass blowers worked at their kilns before twenty foreigners in athletic shoes and cameras standing behind a rope. Dark granite terrace homes were strung around the hills in orderly curves and crowds walked up and down the main commercial streets where pubs advertised bagpipe music and "real" Ceilidh gatherings. A coliseum-like structure stood at the top of the city like a Roman ruin.

At the train station, I asked for directions and set off for a bed and breakfast. The way led me past the big hotels, through a traffic circle and up a churchyard lane. Inside beckoned. My forehead had beads of perspiration as I rang the bell. I was greeted by an unshaven small man with a double chin and an amiable, knowing look. He had a humorous reserve. I asked if anything was available and he rolled his eyes and relented to the resolution of the conflict he had with himself as he set me in a double room.

"O-o-h, it's all we have left, you can have it, normally we like it for two. But you can have it. Same price." He wagged his head a little in friendly disgust. My room was square with tall windows and old fashioned wainscoting. The beds were soft spots in the sensible, sturdy design of the space.

At breakfast I couldn't wait to see the miniature landscape of accouterments on the table. I sat down to a tidily set plate and cutlery, pot of marmalade, coffee cup and saucer, toast rack, butter plate with matching knife, oatcakes in a can, butter, cream, sugar, salt, pepper and a primly folded napkin. It looked like the product of someone's imagination. A bottle of HP brown sauce and ketchup stood on the buffet in case of condiment insufficiency. It all waited in preparation for the arrival of toast, eggs, bacon, porridge and coffee, which I thought might bring the setting to life like Pinocchio. My host sang Baritone snatches in the kitchen and served me in his T-shirt. He looked like he had never left home, as if he let his adolescence slip into middle age because it was just too uncomfortable away from it. We chatted and he mentioned that I should see Tyree.

"Gaelic speakers there. Mull's a good place to walk around with your hands in your pockets. It looks nice. But the Outer Hebrides are more strange."

I told him I was going to Iona.

"That would be nice," he obliged and moved from foot to foot then excused himself to the kitchen.

I paid the bill and stared at the old painted woodwork while a receipt was prepared. Outside I stood by the gate and felt an anxious moment of separation as I left the safety and comfort of the house for a new destination.

The ferry went past enigmatic small islands outside the Oban harbor and landed on Mull. I sat at one of the restaurants in the commercial area that had grown around the ferry landing and had tea served by indifferent waitresses burned out from the tourist trade. My bus came and we drove on a one-lane road through the opaque grey, which settled over the ground. At the extreme west end of the island the rain spattered like vomit as passengers crowded the small toy ferry to Iona for the short crossing. As we bobbed across, the buildings on the Island were strangely visible and bright in the rainy overcast.

"Is anybody going to the Abbey?"

Two women in rain slickers were darting through the crowd as it disembarked to collect members of a group who followed them to a waiting set of vans. I wanted to go to the Abbey and blithely put my stuff in their vans and followed the leader. We walked up a small hill, through an ancient Nunnery without a roof and along an asphalt road to the large stone Abbey set in a yard of vivid wet grass.

Inside we passed a courtyard and continued on into the large dining hall for the complex of buildings. I ate the cake and coffee at the reception for the arrivees, but could no longer retain my innocence when rooms were assigned and my name wasn't on the roster. The woman in charge approached me as I tried to wipe the crumbs of illicit cake from my face and stuff my cup behind me. I hoped she wouldn't be outraged by a little minor theft in a holy place; I really was interested in the Abbey. It wasn't theft anyway, it was embezzlement.

I managed to conceal my venality and get an invitation to lunch the next day. On my way out I stopped in the Abbey bookstore where I milled around the shelves among visitors wearing birkenstocks and little day packs. A short history explained that although the original abbey was attributed to St. Columba, who arrived in five sixty three, the present buildings are much more recent. The Cathedral was restored and reopened in nineteen hundred and five and designed in the shape of a cross seventy by one hundred and sixty feet. Besides the Cathedral Church of Saint Mary, there is the nunnery, a building called the Bishop's House and five Chapels, the oldest of which is St. Oran's. By the outside gate I walked past St. Oran's, located next to a graveyard where kings of Scotland, Ireland and Norway are said to be buried.

The tourists distracted me from the religious presence of these buildings. In addition, I wasn't clear about the doctrine of this Church. It had a monastic tradition but there were no monks around. The visitors were good-natured liberals who seemed more comfortable with discussions about psychology than religious thought.

I walked out into a light rain. It was hard to know the time of day because the light was peculiar to the weather, not the hour. I went around the south side of the island, through the small commercial district and past a rocky beach. At the end of a road curving west the sky lightened and turned into a gradient starting with the earth of deep green, hard marble grey where the sky met the horizon and diffuse white at the top. The low skies intensified the greenness of the grass. I passed a fence and walked over a flat plain surrounded by rocky hills. A bankless brook ran through the turf which ended at short white sand cliffs. Tall rocks washed by the surf stood in contrast to the harmlessness of the beach. The solemnity of the setting was invigorating. It was serious and solemn without being depressive. The green hills seemed to take their life from the ground and complement the sky with their independent power.

I continued up some wet hills where water flowed from an indiscernible source. The tiny island teemed with fresh water, even in the high spots. The direction took me to a knoll overlooking the southern end of the island and down to a road leading to the small town. I ordered a meal in the plain restaurant and watched the third weather front in four hours blow in, coloring the air bronze and pink

At the restaurant, the waitress gave me a three-digit number to call for lodging. Mrs. Black had space and gave me clear instructions I immediately forgot. As I circled a house on a small bluff to see if it was where I wanted to go, a man walked by in the dim light.

"Hello! Is this the Black residence?" I called.

"No, I'm going there though, would you like me to show you?"

"Yes, please."

I walked with the tall man who told me he was part of a group which walked here from Holy Island on the East Coast of England. At Mrs. Black's we entered and I was shown to a generous-sized room with cabin style coziness. Despite the late hour, she made a cold vegetable plate for me, served with homemade preserves and bread. I ate in the privacy of the informal dining room while a new batch of rain pelted the house.

The man from last night was seated erectly in his chair as we waited for toast and coffee to be served. It was sunny and yellow today and sheep wandered around the yard. We greeted each other as I sat down by the window. His long face looked down at the table.

"You're the man from Holy Island," I said.

"Well, sort of, I really come from Manchester, but we started our walk from Holy Island. I didn't get your name, Mine's Tim."

"I'm Bob. Are you any particular denomination?"

"I'm Church of England, but many other churches are represented. You're American, aren't you?" He fussed with his toast.

"Yes, of course."

"Could be Canadian you know, I happen to be dealing with a bunch of Americans at the moment."

"In what capacity?"

"I'm an executive for a large manufacturing firm and we've been put in trusteeship due to a legal problem over the inheritance of the company assets. Family fight you know."

"How does this involve Americans?"

"Well, some of the interested parties are American, and they have had American trust lawyers to represent them over the administrative battle. I have to negotiate with them you see, I'm representing another branch of the family."

"How have you found them, the Americans, I mean?"

"Well, I surprise them, I think."

"How?"

"We have to negotiate a lot about the future of the company, how long it will be, how many employees to keep, etc.. I want to keep more people than they think should be kept. At one point they asked me, 'How can you be in the business if you don't want to run it as efficiently as possible?' or something like that. 'Your ideas will cause it to make less money!' But I told them we will still make more than enough. They blinked and said, 'why are you in this? What for?' It wasn't enough for them to see someone make enough money for all concerned, they wanted *all* the money possible. I told them, 'I'm in it for love, and responsibility to my employees.' Their jaws dropped a meter. This notion did not exist to them. I may as well have told them that I would work for free. They collapsed a little in their expensive black suits and tried to figure out how to deal with someone as deranged as me. Americans run their personal relations like business relations. They don't care about people. I hope I'm not offending you. Are you going to the service tomorrow?"

"Yes." I wasn't sure *I* believed him but he seemed matter of fact about his position.

"How do you like the Island? Are you Church of England?"

"No."

"Hm. What's your interest here?"

"The idea of Immanence and the Druids. They influenced Christianity with the idea that divinity is inside you and you don't need the Catholic-style intervention of a priest for religious experience."

"Can't say. It's a new idea to me."

"I'm looking for a trace of it here. Something left from primitive Scotland. When you look at this vivid little green place, a person can understand how one doesn't need a priest to feel the presence of something special here. The land brings out the mystic in you."

We made conversation with two Scottish girls and reached around the small table for condiments, while Tim spread fastidious layers of margarine and marmalade on his toast.

I awoke from my nap and hurried downstairs to wash my face in the tea-colored water. I was late for lunch at the Abbey and ran through the yard past lounging cats and fleeing chickens towards the road. At the Abbey, lunch was half finished but my hostess set me up at a table at the end of the long hall. An Australian boy in a worn flannel shirt and blue jeans sitting next to me introduced himself and told me he was an architect.

"Australian economy's dead now. It seemed like a good time to travel," he said.

"Seems like a strange place to go when you are out of work. The Australian economy must be bigger than the one on Iona. What do you do here? Are you religious?"

"No, I just work in the kitchens, I started as a volunteer for food and lodging and eventually got put on the paid staff. I have no religious involvement at all."

"Do the people here mind?"

"No, they don't care, this is not a strict place as far as religion goes. You can think what you like."

"What is the point of their beliefs?"

"I'm not sure. They have a center across the way which was founded by the MacCleods to teach the islanders trade skills. That was a while ago. I guess they are generally Christian of some sort. They're nice though, and organized."

"Where else have you been?"

"I went to the Orkneys and the Shetland Islands."

"Were they different than here?"

"A little, one of the little ones still uses the Julian Calendar. They say there's more Scandinavian influence there, but it's mostly played up for the purposes of tourism. The Norwegians controlled the Hebrides for almost the same amount of time as they did the Eastern Islands. There is something though."

"What?"

"There are people there, with dark complexions and narrow eyes. I was told they are proof that the Norsemen went to North America." He paused and brushed his red hair from his forehead.

"How?"

"They are supposed to be descendants of American Indians captured by the Norsemen and brought to the islands." He looked tired from his work and his speech was non-plussed.

"Did you see them?" It sounded like your basic lie.

"Yes, but I couldn't be sure where they were from. I saw some people with kind of Asiatic eyes."

"How could they do that? How can some Viking talk an Indian into going across the mind freezing, uncharted void of the ocean? A person would have to have an intensely developed death wish to go along."

"Forget conversation, maybe they were taken as slaves. Their languages aren't even related. Maybe they just forced them."

The oddness of the idea struck me in the head. I wanted to put down my fork and go immediately to see for myself. I wondered if it was true. He seemed modest. Then I remembered something.

"You know, in central Vermont, a New England state, there are stone huts excavated from solid rock. They are half buried and four to six people can squeeze in them on circular stone benches. When you are inside them it is like being in a granite egg. No one is sure where they came from. The local Indians didn't do that sort of thing. Some people speculate that they were built by people from this area, maybe Irish. It's eerie to sit in them. No one pays attention to them either. No road signs or tours."

"Didn't know that." We paused and looked at our plates for a second. Lunch was over.

"I should go," he said, "Nice to meet you."

Services the next day were packed. I sat on the floor of the chapel using a cushion provided for this purpose. We sang anthem-like hymns with wobbly melodies and recited prayers of indeterminate design. The minister was a regular fellow who started the sermon with an anecdote about an international soccer match.

"Who are these guys?" I kept thinking, "What do they believe?"

They mentioned Christ and heaven and God, but the whole thing was so thin that I stopped paying attention to the service and started flipping through the prayer book. On page twenty-two I accidentally found the most concise statement of belief I could find in the book. It said that they believe in the "Pentecostal fire within" as the source and direction of their religious experience. I stopped and stared. Had I found a connection between these pliable, well meaning liberals and some ancient Celts who were galvanized by the almost pagan significance of the land? In lieu of communion, a loaf of bread and homemade wine was passed around. At the reception I drank tea in the crowd and listened to a woman ask the minister several times if he would hear her confession. Despite his friendly protests that he doesn't take confessions, the woman kept asking in pursuit of her emotional agenda. I eavesdropped on light conversations among the informally dressed crowd. People in hiking boots and bulky sweaters kept nodding and smiling at one another.

At our lodging Tim sat in the chair across from mine and stirred his tea.

"Did you like the service? I found it pleasant," he smiled in my direction.

"No content," I said, "It was barely religious."

Tim was disappointed, "I thought it was nice. You don't prefer dogma do you? Do you want a set of rules and pedantic practices?"

"No, but something other than vague ideas and tolerance without discretion. I want the anger of Old Testament moralists or the choruses of Ukrainian Orthodox churches. Something that reflects a special event that shook people up. I'm not even particular about the religion."

"It's better to accept people for what they are. The service was peaceful and simple. You are judgmental."

"True, but I was bored."

He looked at me with some concern and dipped his narrow face into his cup.

"You're not offended are you?" I asked.

"No, but I worry. I'm the tall worrier." He smiled and winced together. I decided to change the subject to something lighter.

"What are you going to do this evening?" I asked.

"A group of us have a special prayer service tonight at the Chapel. I'm looking forward to it. It will be more intimate than this morning." He forced a smile at me. I really wanted to go.

"That sounds nice." I looked at him and waited for an invitation. He stared at me for a couple of seconds as if I couldn't be thinking what he thought I was thinking.

"It's private, just for our group," he said to make the clear very clear.

That night a spider-like balding man was sitting in the parlor as I came in. He had a ponytail and a deliberate, brooding presence. I turned on the small T.V. and watched a show about fishing in the Zambezi River. He said something about the T.V. and I asked if it was disturbing him. He slowly uncoiled his long legs and shifted in his chair.

"No," he said, "it's just that I used to live in Africa, old Rhodesia."

"What was it like?"

"I like India better, I've been there four times."

I became excited. On the T.V. the man was pulling out surprising, unrecognizable fish while the tall guest was telling me about exotic places.

"Why is it better for you than Africa?" I wanted to know about both. He frowned and stared at the T.V..

"It's part of my personal myth."

Jesus. A new-age catchword. I hoped he didn't start on the power of crystals.

"I don't understand, why myth?"

"You can't explain it, it's part of my voyage on the earth. Do you know Joseph Campbell?"

He looked at me as if I was slightly unevolved and perhaps inadequate to work with these ideas.

"Yes, of course."

"Have you ever been to Findhorn?" he asked.

"No, but I'm interested in it."

"Go there, you will find out more about these things."

He smiled at me, confident that he had projected his enigma.

The next morning I sat with him and his girlfriend from Santa Fe, New Mexico and listened to conversations about Ley lines in England.

"People don't understand them," he fussed, "they think the lines preceded the spots they join, that they were roads or something. But that is not the case, the special spots determined the points on the lines. The lines exist where they do because they had to."

"What's on the spots?" I asked through crumbly toast.

"Abbeys, cairns, standing stones, ponds, anything of traditional sacred significance. The structures were put there because of the energy of the spot. What do you think?"

I had a weakness for this type of speculation.

"I've heard people criticize them and archaeologists don't use them. Some of them even miss the points that determine their lines, like the one that is supposed to run from Stonehenge to Clealing Rings."

He listened to my opinion without rancor then ignored it and started explaining the local landscapes on Iona in terms of "local myth" to Mrs. Black, who came into clean. On the island individual plots of land and prominent features are named in Gaelic on the map. Mrs. Black listened to the expansive explanation meant to include her in our little party, but it barely dented her view of life which focused around work and responsibility for her household. She was too unpretentious to feign interest but was polite and tidied up the parlor as he spoke. When he was done I asked him what his interest in Iona was.

"All these islands are spiritual. Can't you feel it? Why else do you think monks would stay here?"

I was getting confused by the overlapping of religion, popular spirituality and psychology, so I called one of the Church Wardens at the Abbey. Joanna Anderson answered and I told her that I couldn't ascertain the denomination of the Church.

"Well, that's true, we're Ecumenical."

"What's that?"

"Non-denominational, the church was given to us by the Argyle family with the condition that it didn't discriminate."

"I noticed in you prayer book that you mention the inner fire or Pentecostal inner light. I can't remember the exact words. Does this reflect a belief in the idea of Immanence?"

"Yes, it does."

"Can it be traced to Druids?"

"I can't really say, but it can be traced back to the Celtic Christianity that existed here between approximately five hundred and eight hundred A.D.. They had the idea that God exists inside you and around you. For Druidic influences, if they exist, you'd have to check Irish history prior to Columba's departure from Ireland to Iona. The Druids weren't Christians you know."

"Yes, but Christianity has always drawn from philosophical and religious influences besides the Gospels."

"You'd have to check some more. I think Creationist thinking has a more direct relation to our thought though, if you are looking for a historical line."

"So, you people have revived a type of thinking?"

"Yes."

She sounded vaguely suspicious of me.

"Is there any relation between the Abbey and Findhorn?"

"No, none at all. Separate origins. And I'd like to tell you that what I say are my words and not those of the community."

"Yes. O.K.. I'm not trying to trick you."

"Goodbye."

"Goodbye."

I lost three fishing lures as I bumped my way from bank to bank along the Ross of Mull towards the mainland. The third lure waved derisively from its snag in the bottom of a swift stream and I stared at the bare, useless end of my line and wondered how I would continue to poach. Occasional cars passed by on the one lane road so I packed up and stuck my thumb out. For twenty minutes I picked at day-old fish and chips and stared at the high ridges of Central Mull until a van stopped, which forced me to abandon the cold potatoes as I trundled after the car with my pack. A portly middle-aged man made space for my things in the back and we drove on towards the ferry landing.

"Where are you headed?"

"Back to the mainland, near Inverness."

"On holiday?"

"Sort of. I walked across from east to west."

"You must like the Scots."

"Curious."

"Are we as stingy as people say we are? Scots are said to be tight."

"No, people have been cordial."

"We're not greedy. I think we are a country people who save things because replacements aren't convenient. The land around here is rocky and cold. Traditionally we're not wealthy and if you wasted something, it took a long time to get the money to buy another in a town that wasn't close."

"Yes." It sounded right.

"I thought you were walking?"

"East to west was enough. I want to see one or two more places and I'm going by bus."

"What else have you noticed about us?"

"The English are in the back of your mind."

"We don't hate them, you know. People complain about the poll tax, but government thought it would be better than raising the rates. Property taxes. You understand?"

"Yes, I've heard lots about the poll tax."

"The Scots don't really hate anybody nowadays."

Findhorn exists in an almost artificial world of privacy and non-aggression. The unreality of it is enhanced by the juxtaposition of the caravan park and the extensive use of trailers with other architectural styles. I walked up the main road past experimental housing with grass growing on the roofs and back down to a small pizzeria with a medical school diploma on the wall.

"What is this?" I asked.

"It's mine," said a cheerful lithe man with even grey hair.

"What's it doing on the wall?"

"I used to be a doctor in Vancouver, but it got too boring."

"Do you own this place?"

"Yes." He smiled and got into a car to deliver a pizza.

I was left talking with his assistant whose teeth made a white row through his beard. He showed an inordinate interest in my age and became slightly admonishing when I asked questions about the nature of this place.

Just up the road was a bookstore and small whole food grocery. I passed titles on Indian mystics, massage, Lesbian poetry, esoteric Christianity and stone circles in the U.K. on my way to the well-stocked grocery part of the building, where I purchased a huge salad sandwich. The propellers on tall wind generators moved laconically as I leaned against the stairs and ate.

The community center was built in a rustic style with large common rooms and a kitchen. I looked over accommodations listed on the notice board and chose a B and B on the grounds. It turned out to be a small trailer whose owner had a tiny spare room and the price included a cook-it- yourself vegetarian breakfast. When the owner excused herself to go on an errand I looked through her bookshelf which contained titles such as *Sex and Your Spirit Zones*, *Wholeness and the Worlds Beyond*, and *Meditation Techniques*. On her bulletin board were small notes from friends containing Khalil Ghibran-style encouragements and acknowledgments of her spiritual qualities. I wished one of her special gifts was a willingness to make breakfast for her paying guests.

The next day I did laundry for my hostess and myself and wandered around the grounds until lunch in the community center. As I walked I looked for some reason this place started *here*, in sensible, Presbyterian, Scotland. At noon I went through the long table lined with vegetarian dishes and sat at a table with three men in their fifties. They looked like investment bankers on a sailing holiday in their topsiders and khaki pants, and stood out in contrast to the crowd in work clothes and lumpy pullovers. We nodded at one another and I eavesdropped as I stared at my plate.

"My meditation is taking too much time," one of them said.

"Meditate less. You don't have to kill yourself."

"I wonder if I have to do it at all?"

"What choice do you have?"

"You know those tapes, that teach you a language in your sleep? Well maybe we should make one of those."

"Why don't you just get someone to do it for you?"

"Great idea, meditation for pay. I can see it now, meditation services for rent."

"We could specialize and sell tape packages for the different styles!"

"Hey! We could develop meditation space. Don't you get sick of waiting for a room at the center? This is going to be big. Think of the loan origination fees!"

I started laughing and they looked over to me and grinned.

"Be careful what you say, this guy might be an agent from Time or Newsweek."

"No, I'm not an agent, but I have to give you credit. Everyone seems so flaccid here. You're the only ones I've met so far with a sense of irony."

They smiled at each other and said nothing in response. Lunch was almost over.

"We have to go. Where are you from?"

I told them. It turned out we had mutual acquaintances.

"Say 'hi' to Penny and Bob for me." He told me his name.

"Enjoy your stay."

They left in a pack and I walked over to the grocery where the daily tour for visitors was forming.

After introductions our rumpled, accommodating guide took us around the substantial grounds, where we saw the various enterprises on their property. They had a publishing and distribution business, pottery kilns, building techniques courses, organic farming, a coffee house and a wind generator which supplied significant electricity. They also developed organic, environmentally sound products for construction materials. We went to a small meditation hut built of stone into a small bluff. It was a good room despite the pretentious design on the floor. We were told that this was a place for peace and if we wanted to stay for a couple of minutes in silence to "soak up the peace" we could. The group decided it wanted to remain and we sat there for a bit. When it was over some of the group made refreshed noises and nodded to one another. As we went out the door a young girl of about eleven sat in the Lotus position near the entrance with closed eyes and a beatific look. Our guide amiably pointed out the precociousness of the child and the obvious merit of meditation and peace. I got restless. When I was her age, I wanted sex, baseball, and theft from the local variety store. Their influence was misguiding her. I wanted to give her a cigarette and a beer; tell her to get lost and have some fun. And get that look off your face.

At the center we watched an Amway-style tape about the founding of this area. The founder, a woman, had a divine experience which told her to start a garden here. Through introspection, she found guidance and it grew into this organized community. The tape stressed the "inner voice in all of us," while colors swirled on the screen. After the tape was over we asked questions and the guide made it clear that they weren't an isolationist group of cranks, but made it a point to hire adults and adolescents from outside the community. They had no specific religious orientation but were concerned with the maintenance of spiritual life and conservation of the earth.

It was all sensible and the visible signs were of real success. They screened prospective members carefully and didn't have the pathological types that tend to find tolerant groups. What made me uncomfortable about the community was the feeling that the group identity prevailed over individual talent. Pleasant cooperation was the standard rather than inspiration. The only evidence of inner light I found was the guys at the community center joking about meditation. Everybody else was almost extinct. The people were similar to the people I met at the church on Iona and their inclinations seemed the same. Well-meaning people attracted to earth buffered meditation huts, doctrines of the living earth, the divinity in the individual and non-denominational spirituality. Was this an internationalized, conventionalized expression of original Celtic religious identity? It felt un- Scottish. I took a bus towards Edinburgh.

Chapter Ten

Future power

I walked into the plain white offices of the Scottish Nationalist Party expecting to meet an eccentric middle-aged man. Instead, Kevin Pringle was an extremely young man with black hair and an impassive small face. I would be surprised if he was past twenty-five. He had agreed to an interview in his capacity of Research Officer for the SNP, and as we walked to the conference room, we went past rooms staffed by people the same age as Kevin. It looked like a high school newspaper manned by downy-faced adolescents.

Without any ceremony, we took chairs and faced each other. His tie hung loosely from his neck and the patent leather of his shoes was a proletarian touch of flamboyance to his plain, functional presence. His knowledge of the party agenda was in-depth and as we spoke he didn't need notes for his facts and explanations. After rendering a complex analysis he would quietly sit there waiting for my next question and answer it with the same competent, matter-of-fact delivery. I felt his energies went into discipline rather than enthusiastic public relations.

"What are your reasons for wanting independence? You have been part of England for a long time."

"The government of England is a Tory government. By that I mean it's run by old, vested interests such as London aristocracy, industrialists and by businessmen whose center is the south of England. They see Scotland as a resource whose people aren't to be considered as important as those in the south."

"Do you think Independent Scotland would be free of special interest groups?"

"No, but our political culture is different. It's not as elitist and we have more community concern. We tend to think of our surrounding people, our neighbors, more."

"Is it a race thing? Celts vs. Britons vs Anglo Saxons."

"Not really. There's been a lot of mixing. We are different though, but it certainly is not a blood hatred. We aren't anti-English; we don't like Tory traditions. Also it's never going to be equal with sixty million English vs five million Scots."

"What do the English politicians say about your party?"

"It's based on emotionalism and romanticism. They think we are fighting Culloden again, reborn as clansmen. It's not that at all."

"What would you do if independent?"

"First we'd get steel going again. All the industry went south during the eighties when the English privatized and centralized their steel making. Glasgow lost lots of jobs. We would start it up again here and run it publicly; at least to start. Did you know that even with steel at a stand still now, we export more per capita in manufacturing than Germany or Japan? We also aren't afraid of letting foreigners operate and buy businesses here."

"What about water privatization?"

"We oppose it. We feel that private companies will raise rates. Even Thatcher opposed privatization of certain industries."

"You mean industries that tend to be natural monopolies, like gas, telephone, water?"

"Yes."

"Do you have old fashioned nationalist sentiments?"

"No, we want to integrate into the new European model for its community. Its organization gives small states more power than if they act alone. The present union with England is old fashioned and tends towards inequality. We feel political, economic and social rights are more important than independence for its own sake. But it happens that we can't have these things without independence."

"Don't you think it's naive to rely on the European Court to enforce its decisions? Isn't a national military and economic power the best and most reliable means for enforcing agreements? Wouldn't you need England in this regard?"

"No, we anticipate no big power would go beyond the jurisdiction of the court in case of a dispute."

"I've read that you don't like nuclear power."

"Yes, we oppose nuclear facilities in general. We don't want waste treatment plants and we oppose the trident missile system."

"What about treaty organizations?"

"No NATO, and at first no alignments until we saw what was in our best interests. Ultimately we think we'd have to have a special treaty arrangement with the British Isles."

"What problems would you have with the transition to independence?"

"None really, the transition could be very easy. The infrastructure is all in place. We have steel plants, government buildings, established borders, legal system, etc."

"Do you think the English would let you go? You have a lot of valuable things up here."

"John Major himself said that it's Scotland's decision. In his speech to Conservative Parliamentary and District Council Candidates in February of this year he said, 'If Scotland wants independence, it can be done.' Ian Lang, the Scottish Secretary and MP said that if the Scots want independence, they can vote for it and get it. That was on television."

"What about North Sea oil? Would the English let that go quietly?"

"We could negotiate something. Fiscally, its importance is overstated. The one billion in taxes it generates are only one-half of one percent of English tax revenues. We have lots of oil. We could guarantee them a supply."

"But tax revenue isn't the only value the oil has. It pumps money into the national economy and has a multiplier effect. A lot of money went into developing it and the private oil industries would be concerned about its fate. In addition, it's a major export for England. People go to war over things like that."

"We feel we could negotiate something. The nineteen fifty-eight Geneva Continental Shelf Convention provides some guidelines for legal division."

"You say you are a left of center party. What do you do that the Labour Party doesn't do? What need do you fill?"

"Labour proposes regional status within the E.C. as opposed to independence in Europe and that won't work. Regions have no decision making power in the E.C.. The Committee of Regions is part of an advisory body without decisive power. You have to be a member state to have power in the Council of Ministers. We are a nation and must become a member state."

"Do you think that your power would be diminished by joining European integration?"

"No, European integration enhances the power of smaller states such as Denmark, Ireland and Greece."

"What is your popular support like?"

"Polls put us at twenty to twenty-five percent support. In the last general elections we took twenty-one and a half percent of the vote and we are the fastest growing party. Especially among the young and working class."

"What other major concerns do you have?"

"Unemployment, housing. That's why we want to bring back manufacturing and protect our fishing industry better. We're the only ones tying up for eight consecutive days a month to conserve fish. Some of the Outer Hebrides have up to twenty-five percent unemployment. We have to work on these problems with growth and financial planning. By the way, financial services are a huge industry in Scotland today. Depending on how you measure, ours is the second largest in the E.C.. It's not unrealistic to consider putting the European Bank in Edinburgh."

Our time was up. Kevin blinked and waited to see if I wanted anything else. We went into the office where he gave me lots of printed materials and an SNP Position Paper which set out an in depth plan for medium term recovery. As I flipped through it, I saw that it wasn't something you could flip through. The plans were technical with cites and footnotes.

"Wait a second, I want to give you a copy of a recent article." Kevin ran into the copying room. The article, dated April twelfth, 1992, showed that SNP's support rose from fourteen per cent in 1987 to twenty one per cent in the General Election. The author also speculated that most of Labour's constituency might switch to SNP for the district elections. The article was written by a professor of politics at Glasgow University and appeared in the Sunday Times.

I thanked him and went to the train station, where I sat next to a dozing West African and organized my notes. In two hours I was back in Newcastle and looked up an article by Thomas Innes about the history of clans. I was skeptical about Kevin Pringle's "community oriented" description of Scots. It sounded like sugar coated propaganda. "The Highland clan, or lowland 'name' both provided a closely knit community, in which all clansmen, however humble...took pride in clan history and felt themselves to be, like the chief, descended from the founder ancestor. It was a society without humiliating class distinctions, wherein rank and titles of the chief were a source of pride to all. In fact a considerable number, sometimes a majority of the clansmen, were descended from the tribal chiefs."

I didn't believe it, so I read another article by Ms. I.F. Grant, a reputable Scottish historian:

"The key institution in holding the clans together as a cohesive community was the chiefship.... His policies, in fact, had to accord in a general way with the sentiment of the body. At all events, his power derived from his prestige as heir of the clan founder and as the legal landlord of the clan lands and not upon any personal army or police force. So that it was impossible for him to become a tyrant.... He was the father of his clan and looked after the welfare of his clansmen, including provisions for the care of the ill and indigent. He saw that the clan lands were distributed so as to provide a living for all."

I put down my book and frowned. People caring about each other? Hard to believe. Maybe it was my American upbringing. I got up and phoned the travel agent in London for a return flight to America.

"We have the days you need, from where would you like to depart?"

"London is fine."

"You're in Newcastle, let me check something else. Maybe a departure closer to you." I waited.

"We have London, and Glasgow."

"Glasgow is closer than London, I think."

"Yes, an hour, or so," the agent laughed, "I hope you don't mind people who smell like whiskey."